TERRY EAGLETON was born in Salford in 1943. He was educated at local schools and at Cambridge University where he became a Fellow in English. In 1969 he became Fellow and Tutor at Wadham College, Oxford. His publications include: *Shakespeare and Society* (1967), *Exiles and Emigres* (1970), *Myths of Power: A Marxist Study of the Brontës* (1976), *Criticism and Ideology* (Verso/NLB 1976), and *Walter Benjamin or Towards a Revolutionary Criticism* (Verso/NLB 1981).

Terry Eagleton

The Function of Criticism

From *The Spectator* to Post-Structuralism

Verso is the imprint of **New Left Books**

British Library
Cataloguing in Publication Data

Eagleton, Terry
The Function of Criticism
1. Criticism — Social aspects — England
2. Criticism — England — History
I. Title
801'.95'0942   PN99.G7

First published 1984
© Terry Eagleton 1984
Second impression 1985
Third impression 1987
Fourth impression 1990
Fifth impression 1991

Verso
UK: 6 Meard Street, London W1V 3HR
USA: 29 West 35th Street, New York, NY 10001 2291

Filmset in Palatino by
PRG Graphics
Redhill, Surrey

Printed in Great Britain by
Dotesios Ltd, Trowbridge, Wiltshire

ISBN 0 86091 091 1
        0 86091 779 1 Pbk

til

Toril

min kjaereste venn

Preface

Perhaps I could best describe the impulse behind this book by imagining the moment in which a critic, sitting down to begin a study of some theme or author, is suddenly arrested by a set of disturbing questions. What is the *point* of such a study? Who is it intended to reach, influence, impress? What functions are ascribed to such a critical act by society as a whole? A critic may write with assurance as long as the critical institution itself is thought to be unproblematical. Once that institution is thrown into radical question, then one would expect individual acts of criticism to become troubled and self-doubting. The fact that such acts continue today, apparently in all their traditional confidence, is doubtless a sign that the crisis of the critical institution has either not been deeply enough registered, or is being actively evaded.

The argument of this book is that criticism today lacks all substantive social function. It is either part of the public relations branch of the literary industry, or a matter wholly internal to the academies. That this has not always been the case, and that it need not even today be the case, I try to show by a drastically selective history of the institution of criticism in England since the early eighteenth century. The guiding concept of this brief survey is that of the 'public sphere', first developed by Jurgen Habermas in his *Structural Transformation of the Public Sphere* (1962). This concept has proved by no means uncontroversial: it hovers indecisively between ideal model and historical description, suffers from severe problems of historical periodization, and in Habermas's own work is not easily dissociable from a certain view of socialism which is deeply debatable. The 'public sphere' is a notion difficult to rid of nostalgic, idealizing connotations; like the 'organic society', it sometimes seems to have been disintegrating since its inception. It is not my intention here, however, to enter into these theoretical contentions; I am concerned rather to deploy aspects of the concept, flexibly and opportunistically, to shed light on a particular history. It goes without saying that this historical retrospect is by no means politically disinterested: I examine this history as a way of raising the question of what substantive social functions criticism might once again fulfil in our own time, beyond its crucial role of maintaining from within the academies a critique of ruling-class culture.

I must thank in particular Perry Anderson, John Barrell, Neil Belton, Norman Feltes, Toril Moi, Francis Mulhern, Graham Pechey and Bernard Sharratt, all of whom have given me valuable assistance with this book. I am also deeply indebted to the warmth and comradeship of Terry Collits and David Bennett of the University of Melbourne, in whose company I first rehearsed some of these ideas.

T.E.

The Function of Criticism

I

Modern European criticism was born of a struggle against the absolutist state. Within that repressive regime, in the seventeenth and eighteenth centuries, the European bourgeoisie begins to carve out for itself a distinct discursive space, one of rational judgement and enlightened critique rather than of the brutal ukases of an authoritarian politics. Poised between state and civil society, this bourgeois 'public sphere', as Jürgen Habermas has termed it, comprises a realm of social institutions – clubs, journals, coffee houses, periodicals – in which private individuals assemble for the free, equal interchange of reasonable discourse, thus welding themselves into a relatively cohesive body whose deliberations may assume the form of a powerful political force.[1] A polite, informed public opinion pits itself against the arbitrary diktats of autocracy; within the translucent space of the public sphere it is supposedly no longer social power, privilege and tradition which confer upon individuals the title to speak and judge, but the degree to which they are constituted as discoursing subjects by sharing in a consensus of universal reason. The norms of such reason, while in their own way absolute, turn their backs upon the insolence of aristocratic authority; the rules, as Dryden remarks, are 'founded upon good sense, and sound reason, rather

9

than on authority.[2]

'In the Age of Enlightenment,' writes Peter Hohendahl, 'the concept of criticism cannot be separated from
the institution of the public sphere. Every judgement is
designed to be directed toward a public; communication
with the reader is an integral part of the system. Through
its relationship with the reading public, critical reflection loses its private character. Criticism opens itself to
debate, it attempts to convince, it invites contradiction.
It becomes a part of the public exchange of opinions.
Seen historically, the modern concept of literary criticism is closely tied to the rise of the liberal, bourgeois
public sphere in the early eighteenth century. Literature
served the emancipation movement of the middle class
as an instrument to gain self-esteem and to articulate its
human demands against the absolutist state and a hierarchical society. Literary discussion, which had previously served as a form of legitimation of court society
in the aristocratic salons, became an arena to pave the
way for political discussion in the middle classes.'[3] This
process, Hohendahl goes on to remark, happened first in
England; but one should stress that, given the peculiari-
ties of the English, the bourgeois public sphere was
consolidated more in the wake of political absolutism
than as a resistance to it from within. The English
bourgeois public sphere of the early eighteenth century,
of which Steele's *Tatler* and Addison's *Spectator* are central institutions, is indeed animated by moral correction
and satiric ridicule of a licentious, socially regressive
aristocracy; but its major impulse is one of class-
consolidation, a codifying of the norms and regulating of
the practices whereby the English bourgeoisie may
negotiate an historic alliance with its social superiors.
When Macaulay remarks that Joseph Addison 'knew
how to use ridicule without abusing it', he means in

effect that Addison knew how to upbraid the traditional ruling class while keeping in with it, avoiding the divisive vituperation of a Pope or Swift. Jurgen Habermas points out that the public sphere develops earlier in England than elsewhere because the English gentry and aristocracy, traditionally involved in questions of cultural taste, also shared economic interests with the emergent mercantile class, unlike, say, their French counterparts. The intimacy of cultural, political and economic preoccupations is thus more marked in England than elsewhere. The hallmark of the English public sphere is its consensual character: the *Tatler* and *Spectator* are catalysts in the creation of a new ruling bloc in English society, cultivating the mercantile class and uplifting the profligate aristocracy. The single daily or thrice-weekly sheets of these journals, with their hundreds of lesser imitators, bear witness to the birth of a new discursive formation in post-Restoration England – an intensive intercourse of class-values which 'fuse(d) the best qualities of Puritan and Cavalier' (A.J. Beljame) and fashioned 'an idiom for common standards of taste and conduct' (Q.D.Leavis). Samuel Johnson was to trace this ideological osmosis in Addison's very literary style, 'familiar, but not coarse' as he found it. The moderate Whiggism of Addison and Steele, the unbuttoned, affably non-sectarian quality of a politics which could indulge the backwoods Tory Sir Roger de Coverley even as it admired the Whig merchant Sir Andrew Freeport, underlay this cultural consensus. Addison himself had both city investments and a country estate, reconciling landed and monied interests in his own person; he was, according to one of his commentators, 'his party's most eloquent apologist for English mercantile success and the Exchange', [4] but the Spectator club is deliberately designed to reflect all respectable social ranks (*Spectator*

34). Addison, Beljame effuses, 'fixed his eyes not on the Court alone, but on society as a whole, and he sought to open Everyman's eyes to literature; better still, to open his mind, form his judgement, teach him to think and provide him with general ideas on art and life. He made it his business to conduct a course on literature and aesthetics.'[5] What will help to unify the English ruling bloc, in short, is culture; and the critic is the chief bearer of this historic task.

One might claim, then, that modern criticism in England was born ironically of political consensus. It is not, of course, that the eighteenth century was any stranger to strife and rancour, or that we should imagine the bourgeois public sphere as an organic society of universal agreement. But the ferocious contentions of essayists and pamphleteers took place within the gradual crystallization of an increasingly self-confident ruling bloc in English society, which defined the limits of the acceptably sayable. Leslie Stephen contrasts the oppositional character of such French eighteenth-century men of letters as Voltaire and Rousseau with such critics as Samuel Johnson, who largely shared and articulated the views of the public for whom they wrote.[6] This, indeed, is the irony of Enlightenment criticism, that while its appeal to standards of universal reason signifies a resistance to absolutism, the critical gesture itself is typically conservative and corrective, revising and adjusting particular phenomena to its implacable model of discourse. Criticism is a reformative apparatus, scourging deviation and repressing the transgressive; yet this juridical technology is deployed in the name of a certain historical emancipation. The classical public sphere involves a discursive reorganization of social power, redrawing the boundaries between social classes as divisions between those who engage in rational argument, and those who do not. The sphere of cultural discourse and the realm of social power are closely related but not homologous: the former cuts across and suspends the distinctions of the latter, deconstructing and reconstituting it in a new form, temporarily transposing its 'vertical' gradations onto a 'horizontal' plane. 'In principle,' Hohendahl comments, 'social privileges were not acknowledged whenever private citizens gathered together as a public body. In the reading societies and clubs, status was suspended so that a discussion among equals could take place. Authoritarian, aristocratic art judgements were replaced 18THC by a discourse among educated laymen.'[7] A new cultural formation is mapped on to the traditional power-structure of English society, momentarily dissolving its distinctions in order the more thoroughly to buttress its hegemony. In the coffee houses of eighteenth-century England (and there were over three thousand of them in London alone), 'the writers rubbed shoulders, in an egalitarian context, with their patrons, whether they were noblemen or squires or parsons or merchants or professional men . . . It is a mark of the literary societies of the age that membership was entirely heterogeneous, including politicians, diplomats, lawyers, theologians, scientists, physicians, surgeons, actors, and so on, besides the poets and other writers.'[8] 'The coffee houses,' Beljame writes, 'provided rallying points. People met, exchanged opinions, formed groups, gathered number. It was through them, in short, that a public opinion began to evolve, which thereafter had to be reckoned with.'[9] Addison, according to his Victorian biographer, was the 'chief architect of Public Opinion in the eighteenth century'.[10] Discourse becomes a political force: 'The spread of general culture in every direction,' remarks the enraptured Beljame, 'united all classes of society. Readers were no longer segregated into water-tight compartments of Puritan and Cavalier, Court and City, the metropolis and province: *all the English were now readers*.[11] He exaggerates a little, no doubt: the *Spectator* sold around three thousand copies in a total population of some five and a half million, the book-buying public of the time can be measured in tens of thousands, and a great many of the English were illiterate or barely literate. It does not seem that the emulsive space of the public sphere extended beyond parsons and surgeons to farm labourers or domestic servants, despite Defoe's surely exaggerated claim that 'you'll find very few Coffee-houses in this opulent City (London), without an illiterate Mechanick, Commenting upon the most material Occurrences, and Judging the Actions of the greatest in *Europe*, and rarely a Victualing House but you meet with a *Tinker*, a *Cobbler*, or a *Porter*, Criticizing upon the Speeches of Majesty, or the writings of the most celebrated Men of the Age.'[12] Nevertheless, Beljame has in his own way grasped the essential point: what is at stake, in this ceaseless circulation of polite discourse among rational subjects, is the cementing of a new power bloc at the level of the sign. The 'advocating of good Literature in the World', according to John Clarke, 'is not only highly subservient to the Ends of Religion and Virtue, but likewise to those of Good Policy and Civil Government.' 'Promotion of good Taste in poetical Compositions,' wrote Thomas Cooke, 'is the Promotion likewise of good Manners. Nothing can more nearly concern a State than the Encouragement of good Writers.'[13]

What is spoken or written, within this rational space, pays due deference to the niceties of class and rank; but the speech act itself, the *énonciation* as opposed to the *énoncé*, figures in its very form an equality, autonomy and reciprocity at odds with its class-bound content. The very act of utterance discloses a quasi-transcendental community of subjects, a universal model of rational exchange, which threatens to contradict the hierarchies and exclusions of which it speaks. The public sphere in some sense resolves the contradictions of mercantile society by boldly inverting its terms: if what is embarrassing for bourgeois liberal theory is the process by which an abstract equality at the level of natural rights becomes transmuted into a system of actual differential rights, the bourgeois public sphere will take those differential rights as its starting-point and convert them back, in the region of discourse, to an abstract equality. The truly free market is that of cultural discourse itself, within, of course, certain normative regulations; the role of the critic is to adminster those norms, in a double refusal of absolutism and anarchy. What is said derives its legitimacy neither from itself as message nor from the social title of the utterer, but from its conformity as a statement with a certain paradigm of reason inscribed in the very event of saying. One's title as a speaker is derived from the formal character of one's discourse, rather than the authority of that discourse derived from one's social title. Discursive identities are not pre-given, but constructed by the very act of participation in polite conversation; and this, one might claim, is to some degree at odds with Lockeian wisdom, for which pre-established propertied subjects then enter into contractual relations with one another. The public sphere, by contrast, acknowledges no given rational identity beyond its own bounds, for what counts as rationality is precisely the capacity to articulate within its constraints; the rational are those capable of a certain mode of discourse, but this cannot be judged other than in the act of deploying it. To collaborate in the public sphere thus becomes the criterion of one's right to do so, though it is of course inconceivable that those without property – without, in the eighteenth-century sense, an 'interest' – could participate in this realm. It is not, however, that the public sphere exists for the direct discussion of those interests; on the contrary, such interests become its very concealed problematic, the very enabling structure of its disinterested enquiry. Only those with an interest can be disinterested. Shadowing all particular utterances within this space, delivered inseparably along with them as the very guarantee of their authority, is the form and event of universal reason itself, ceaselessly reproduced in a style of enunciation and exchange which rises above and sits in judgement upon the partial, local messages it communicates. All utterances thus move within a regime which raises them at the very point of production to universal status, inscribes within them a legitimacy which neither wholly pre-exists the particular statement nor is exactly reducible to it, but which, like the elusive concept of 'capacity', is at once identical with and in excess of whatever is spoken. The very rule-governed form of utterance and exchange is what regulates the relation between individual statements and the discursive formation as a whole; and this form is neither externally imposed by some extrinsic centre, as the state might regulate commodity production, nor wholly organic to the statement itself. The bourgeoisie thus discovers in discourse an idealized image of its own social relations: the 'Literati of the Country', D'Israeli remarks in his *Periodical Essays* (1780), 'are set of independent *Free Burghers*, among whom there is a natural and political equality'.[14] It is not for nothing that Goldsmith noted the significance of the phrase 'republic of letters'; for what could better correspond to the bourgeoisie's dream of freedom than a society of petty producers whose endlessly available, utterly inexhaustible commodity is discourse itself, equitably exchanged in a mode which reconfirms the autonomy of each producer? Only in this ideal discursive sphere is exchange without domination possible; for to persuade is not to dominate, and to carry one's opinion is more an act of collaboration than of competition. Circulation can proceed here without a breath of exploitation, for there are no subordinate social classes within the public sphere – indeed in principle, as we have seen, no social classes at all. What is at stake in the public sphere, according to its own ideological self-image, is not power but reason. Truth, not authority, is its ground, and rationality, not domination, its daily currency. It is on this radical dissociation of politics and knowledge that its entire discourse is founded; and it is when this dissociation becomes less plausible that the public sphere will begin to crumble.

The periodicals of the early eighteenth century were a primary constituent of the emergent bourgeois public sphere. They were, as A.S. Collins writes, 'a very powerful educative influence, affecting politics as well by the formation of a broad, national public opinion'.[15] Jane Jack views the periodicals, with their 'high-class popularization', as the dominant literary form of the first half of the century,[16] and Leslie Stephen described them as 'the most successful innovation of the day'.[17] The *Tatler* and *Spectator* marked a qualitative development from what had come before: 'A number of earlier periodicals,' reports Richard P. Bond, 'had been heavily committed to learned works, using abstracts and extracts more than original criticism, and a few papers had admitted bellelettristic features, but no journal had attempted to elevate taste by giving large attention to the arts, mainly literary, in a way both serious and genial. The *Tatler* was the first English periodical to do this.'[18] It was still not, of course, 'professional' criticism in the modern sense. Steele's own literary comments are *ad hoc* and impressionistic, lacking any theoretical structure or governing principles; Addison is somewhat more analytical, but his criticism, like his thought in general, is essentially empiricist and affective in the mould of Hobbes and Locke, concerned with the pragmatic psychological effect of literary works – does this please, and how? – rather than with more technical or theoretical questions. Literary criticism as a whole, at this point, is not yet an autonomous specialist discourse, even though more technical forms of it exist; it is rather one sector of a general ethical humanism, indissociable from moral, cultural and religious reflection. The *Tatler* and *Spectator* are projects of a bourgeois cultural politics whose capacious, blandly homogenizing language is able to encompass art, ethics, religion, philosophy and everyday life; there is here no question of a 'literary critical' response which is not wholly determined by an entire social and cultural ideology. Criticism here is not yet 'literary' but 'cultural': the examination of literary texts is one relatively marginal moment of a broader enterprise which explores attitudes to servants and the rules of gallantry, the status of women and familial affections, the purity of the English language, the character of conjugal love, the psychology of the sentiments and the laws of the toilet. A parallel range is discernible in Defoe's contemporaneous, vastly influential *Review*, the 'first eminent essay periodical in England to treat politics, economics, ecclesiastical, social and ethical themes'.[19] The critic, as cultural strategist rather than literary expert, must resist specialization: 'The Truth of it is,' Addison remarks in *Spectator* 291, 'there is nothing more absurd, than for a Man to set himself up as a Critick, without a good Insight into all the Parts of Learning . . . ' The polite is at war with the pedantic: though Addison was an enthusiast for scientific experiment and the new philosophy, he espoused such pursuits only because he considered them fit study for a gentleman. The critic as cultural commentator acknowledges no inviolable boundary between one idiom and another, one field of social practice and the next; his role is to ramble or idle among them all, testing each against the norms of that general humanism of which he is the bearer. The flexible, heterogeneous forms of the magazine and periodical reflect this relaxed capaciousness: fictional and non-fictional materials equably co-exist, moral essays slip easily into anecdote and allegory, and the collaboration of the readership is actively solicited in the writing. (In danger of running out of material, Steele at one point warns his audience that unless they write in the journal, it will have to close.) The frontiers between literary genres, as between authors and readers, or genuine and fictitious correspondents, are comfortably indeterminate; the *Tatler* and *Spectator* are themselves complex refinements and recyclings of previous periodical forms, borrowing a device here, polishing or discarding a style there, artfully recombining elements from a number of discrete sources. The digest or abstract of learned books carried for busy readers by some seventeenth-century periodicals (the earliest 'literary criticism' in England, no doubt) has now become elaborated into the full-blown literary critical essay; the bawdy and doggerel of such earlier publications is soberly expunged, but their efforts to disseminate knowledge become in the hands of Addison and Steele a more obliquely informative portrayal of the *beau monde*. The collaborative gambits of such influential journals as John Dunton's *Athenian Mercury*, supplying quasi-scientific answers to readers' inquiries, are modulated to the inclusion of readers' real or fictive correspondence. The seventeenth-century popular press's canny responsiveness to audience demand, feeding its appetite for scientific knowledge, moral solace and social orientation, is preserved, but sublimed to a sophisticated idiom which flatters its readers' *savoir faire* even as it fosters it. Writer and reader, fact and fiction, documentation and didacticism, suavity and sobriety: a single, scrupulously standardised language is constructed to articulate all of these together, blurring the boundaries between production and consumption, reflection and reportage, moral theory and social practice. What emerges from this melting pot of literary sub-genres, class styles and ideological motifs is a new brand of cultural politics, at once broadly dispersed, instantly available and socially closed.

The critic as *flâneur* or *bricoleur*, rambling and idling among diverse social landscapes where he is everywhere at home, is still the critic as judge; but such judgement should not be mistaken for the censorious verdicts of an Olympian authority. 'It is a particular Observation I have always made,' writes Steele in *Tatler* 29, 'That of all Mortals, a Critick is the silliest; for by inuring himself to examine all Things, whether they are of Consequence or not, he never looks upon any Thing but with a Design of passing Sentence upon it; by which means, he is never a Companion, but always a Censor . . . A thorough Critick is a Sort of Puritan in the polite World . . . ' The very act of criticism, in short, poses a pressing ideological problem: for how is one to criticize without lapsing into exactly that sullen sectarianism which has lain waste the English social order, and which it is part of Steele's project genially to reform? How can the ineluctably negative movement of criticism celebrate an ideological compact with the object of its disapprobation?

The very business of criticism, with its minatory over-
tones of conflict and dissension, offers to disrupt the
consensualism of the public sphere; and the critic himself, who stands at the nub of that sphere's great circuits
of exchange, disseminating, gathering in and recircula-
ting its discourse, represents a potentially fractious
element within it. Steele's comforting response to this
dilemma is 'companionship': the critic is less the casti-
gator of his fellows than their clubbable, co-discoursing
equal, spokesman rather than scourge. As passing
symbolic representative of the public realm, the mere
fold of its self-knowledge, he must chide and correct
from within a primordial social pact with his readership,
laying claim to no status or subject position which is not
spontaneously precipitated by those intimate social
relations. ·

Periodical literature, William Hazlitt remarks, is 'in
morals and manners what the experimental is in natural
philosophy, as opposed to the dogmatical method'.[20]
The distinctive tones of the *Tatler* and *Spectator*, light,
eirenic and urbane at the very point of satiric ridicule,
are the sign of this solution. 'In principle,' writes Hohendahl, 'everyone has a basic judgemental capacity,
although individual circumstances may cause each
person to develop that capacity to a different degree.
This means that everyone is called upon to participate in
criticism; it is not the privilege of a certain social class or
professional clique. It follows that the critic, even a professional one, is merely a speaker from the general
audience and formulates ideas that could be thought by
anyone. His special task vis-à-vis the public is to conduct the general discussion.'* Pope treated the same
problem a little more succinctly: 'Men must be taught as
if you taught them not,/And things unknown propos'd
as things forgot' (*Essay on Criticism*). What makes criti-

21

cism's tacit assumption of superiority tolerable, as what makes the accumulation of power and property tolerable, is the fact that all men possess the capacity for it. If such a capacity involves the most civilized skills, it is also incurably amateur: criticism belongs with a traditional English conception of gentility which troubles the distinction between innate and acquired, art and Nature, specialist and spontaneous. Such amateurism is not ignorance or half-capacity, but the casual polymorphous expertise of one to whom no sector of cultural life is alien—who passes from writer to reader, moralist to mercantilist, Tory to Whig and back, offering himself as little more than the vacant space within which these diverse elements may congregate and interbreed. The drawing together of writer and reader, critic and citizen, multiple literary modes and dispersed realms of enquiry, all folded into a language at once mannerly and pellucid, is the mark of a non-specialism which is perhaps only in part intelligible to us today, predating as it does that intellectual division of labour to which our own amateurisms are inevitably reactive. The critic, anyway, as functionary, mediator, chairperson, locus of languages he receives rather than invents; the *Spectator*, as T.H. Green remarked, as a kind of literature which 'consists in talking to the public about itself',[21] and the critic as the mirror in which this fascinated self-imaging takes shape. Regulator and dispensor of a general humanism, guardian and instructor of public taste, the critic must fulfil these tasks from within a more fundamental responsibility as reporter and informer, a mere mechanism or occasion by which the public may enter into deeper imaginary unity with itself. The *Tatler* and *Spectator* are consciously educating a socially heterogeneous public into the universal forms of reason, taste and morality, but their judgements are not to be whimsically authoritarian, the diktats of a technocratic caste. On the contrary, they must be moulded and constrained from within by the very public consensus they seek to nurture. The critic is not in our sense an intellectual: in the eighteenth century, as Richard Rorty comments, 'there were witty men and learned men and pious men, but there were no highbrows'.[22] If, like the silent Mr. Spectator, the critic stands a little apart from the bustle of the metropolis, this is no mark of alienation: it is only so as the more keenly to observe, and so the more effectively to report what he learns of that world to its more preoccupied participants. Valid critical judgement is the fruit not of spiritual dissociation but of an energetic collusion with everyday life. It is in intimate empirical engagement with the social text of early-bourgeois England that modern criticism first makes its appearance; and the line from this vigorous empiricism to F.R. Leavis, along which such criticism will at a certain point mutate into the 'literary', remains relatively unbroken.

Such 'spontaneous' engagements were made possible only by a peculiarly close interaction between the cultural, political and economic. The early eighteenth-century coffee houses were not only forums where, as one commentator puts it, 'a sort of communal reading became the rage';[23] they were also nubs of finance and insurance, where the stockjobbers set up in business and the South Sea Bubble débacle was to reach its climax. In the clubs based on these ambivalently cultural and pragmatic institutions, what Leslie Stephen calls a 'characteristic fraternization of the politicians and the authors' was daily current. Such men, Stephen notes, would congregate at the coffee houses 'in a kind of tacit confederation of clubs to compare notes and form the whole public opinion of the day'.[24] 'Cultural' and political idioms continuously inter-penetrated: Addison himself was a functionary of the state apparatus as well as a journalist, and Steele also held government office. Relations between the literary and political castes were probably closer than at any other point in modern English history, and Thomas Macaulay suggests one plausible reason why this was so. In the early eighteenth century, before the advent of free parliamentary reporting, the effects of parliamentary oratory were limited to its immediate audience; to disseminate ideas beyond this forum thus demanded that intensive political polemicizing and pamphleteering which absorbs so much of the period's literary production. 'It may well be doubted,' Macaulay comments, 'whether St John did so much for the Tories as Swift and whether Cowper did so much for the Whigs as Addison.'[25] If the *Tatler* and *Spectator* are not themselves especially 'political', the cultural project they represent could nevertheless be sustained only through a close traffic with political power; and if they were not especially political, it is in part because, as I have argued, what the political moment demanded was precisely 'cultural'.

'Addison,' writes Macaulay in a celebrated comment, 'reconciled wit with virtue, after a long and disastrous separation, during which wit had been led astray by profligacy and virtue by fanaticism.'[26] The names of Addison and Steele signify the very essence of English compromise: that adroit blending of grace and *gravitas*, urbanity and morality, correction and consolidation could not fail to seduce a later bourgeois intelligentsia, now spiritually severed from the industrial capitalism which had produced them. To return in spirit to a *pre-industrial* bourgeoisie, whose moral fervour has not yet been struck leaden by industrial philistinism, and which sounds the aristocratic note at the same time as it refuses its frivolity: such a fantasy solution, one suspects, would probably have been invented if it had not been historically available. 'There is nothing here as yet,' comment Legouis and Cazamian, 'of that Philistinism with which the English middle classes will be charged later, and not without some reason.'[27] In these early periodicalists, English criticism is able to glimpse its own glorious origins, seize the fragile moment at which the bourgeoisie entered into respectability before passing out of it again. Most literary critics, Raymond Williams once remarked, are natural cavaliers; but since most of them are also products of the middle class, the image of Addison and Steele allows them to indulge their anti-bourgeois animus on gratifyingly familiar, impeccably 'moral' terrain. If Addison and Steele mark the moment of bourgeois respectability, they also signify the point at which the hitherto disreputable genre of journalism becomes legitimate. Previous periodicals, writes Walter Graham, 'suffered from the ills of partisan truculence, rampant sectarianism, crude taste, and personal rancour . . . Thanks to Addison and Steele, the "literary" periodical becomes respectable, and with essay writing, journalism begins to lose its stigma.'[28] The respite from sectarian truculence – one which, as we shall see, was destined to be brief – is identical with the rebirth of the periodical as Literature: it is when writing succeeds in transmuting the sordidly political into 'style', replacing rancour with reconciliation, that it qualifies for the canon. It is for this reason that the eighteenth-century Tory satirists have often proved something of an embarrassment, in their 'extremist' violence, to the later custodians of the literary: are not Swift's prose and *The Dunciad* marred as artefacts by their pathological spleen? The literary is the vanishing point of the political, its dissolution and reconstitution into polite letters. The irony of such a judgement on the eighteenth century is surely plain: the transition from sectarian polemic to cultural consensus which marks the polite periodicals is precisely their most politically essential function.

In the early eighteenth century, then, the bourgeois principle of abstract free and equal exchange is elevated from the market-place to the sphere of discourse, to mystify and idealize real bourgeois social relations. The petty proprietors of a commodity known as 'opinion' assemble together for its regulated interchange, at once miming in purer, non-dominative form the exchanges of bourgeois economy, and contributing to the political apparatus which sustains it. The public sphere thereby constructed is at once universal and class-specific: all may in principle participate in it, but only because the class-determined criteria of what counts as significant participation are always unlodgeably in place. The currency of this realm is neither title nor property but rationality – a rationality in fact articulable only by those with the social interests which property generates. But because that rationality is not the possession of a *single* class within the hegemonic social bloc – because it is the product of an intensive conversation *between* those dominant classes, a discourse for which the *Tatler* and *Spectator* are particular names – it is possible to view it as universal, and hence to prise the definition of the gentleman free of any too rigidly genetic or class-specific determinants. The possession of power and property inserts you into certain forms of polite discourse, but that discourse is by no means merely instrumental to the furtherance of material ends. On the contrary, the communication into which you enter with your equally propertied interlocutors is in an important sense 'phatic': a deployment of the appropriate forms and conventions of discourse which has as its goal nothing more than the delightful exercise of taste and reason. Culture, in this sense, is autonomous of material interests; where it inter-locks with them is visible in the very form of the discursive community itself, in the freedom, autonomy and equality of the speech acts appropriate to bourgeois subjects.

II

The bourgeois public sphere of early eighteenth-century England is perhaps best seen not as a single homogenous formation, but as an interlaced set of discursive centres. The collaborative literary relations established by the *Tatler* and *Spectator* find a resonance elsewhere, though with a markedly different ideological tone, in the writings of Samuel Richardson. I have described elsewhere how Richardson's perpetual circulation of texts among friends and correspondents, with its attendant wranglings, pleadings, revisions, interpretations of interpretations, comes to constitute an entire discursive community of its own, a kind of public sphere in miniaturized or domesticated form within which, amidst all the petty frictions and anxieties of hermeneutical intercourse, a powerfully cohesive body of moral thought, a collective sensibility, comes to crystallize.[29] But it is also relevant in this respect to think of the subscription publishing of Pope and others, which converted readers into collective patrons and transformed their otherwise passive, 'nuclear' relation to the text into membership of a community of benevolent participants in the writing project. Such a writer, like Richardson, actively constructed his own audience: Pope's campaign for subscribers, Pat Rogers has argued, led him to define, to woo, ultimately to create his own readership.[30] Susan Staves has pointed out how 'the new class of the polite is visible in Pope's subscription lists – lords, private gentlemen, doctors, lawyers, bankers, publishers, actors, ladies – mingled together in lists partly alphabetical, partly by rank, all subscribers being grouped by the initial letter of their last names and then, roughly, by rank within each letter.'[31] Distinctions of rank are here preserved, in contrast to the ideal of the public sphere proper, but preserved within the levelling community of the surname initial. Pope, Staves claims, was thus 'participating in the formation of that new, mixed class whose names are displayed in his printed subscription lists'; as the eighteenth century wears on, the vital social distinction 'was not between aristocrats and commoners but between ladies and gentlemen, on the one hand, and the vulgar on the other.' Pope's subscription technique, according to Leslie Stephen, meant that he 'received a kind of commission from the upper class' to execute his work; the traditional individual patron was superseded by a 'kind of joint-stock body of collective patronage'.[32]

As the eighteenth century drew on, the rapid expansion of the forces of literary production began to outstrip and overturn the social relations of production within which such projects as the early periodicals had flourished. By the 1730s, literary patronage was already on the wane, with a concomitant increase in bookseller power; with the expansion of wealth, population and education, technological developments in printing and publishing and the growth of a middle class eager for literature, the small reading public of Addison's day, largely confined to fashionable London, was spawning to support a whole caste of professional writers. By about mid-century, then, the profession of letters had become established and literary patronage was in its death throes; this period witnesses a marked quickening of literary production, a widespread diffusion of science and letters and, in the 1750s and '60s, a veritable explosion of literary periodicals. Samuel Johnson estimated Edmund Cave's *Gentleman's Magazine* to have a circulation of some 10,000; Ian Watt regards such hybrid, non-traditional forms as helping to nurture the public which will devour the novel.[33] Writing, Daniel Defoe noted in 1725, ' . . . is becoming a very considerable Branch of the English Commerce. The Booksellers are the Master Manufacturers or Employers. The several Writers, Authors, Copyers, Sub-Writers and all other operators with Pen and Ink are the workmen employed by the said Master-Manufacturers.'[34] The name Grub Street should warn us against any too deteriorationist a reading of eighteenth-century literary production, as though the golden age of the public sphere was succeeded by a catastrophic fall into commerce; the Grub Street hacks are the contemporaries of Addison and Steele, not their inheritors. Even so, it is possible to trace an intensifying penetration of capital into literary production as the century unfolds; and the celebrated prose style of the epoch's major critic, Samuel Johnson, can be seen as obliquely related to this material development.

Johnson's style, which William Hazlitt described as a 'species of rhyming in prose' ('each sentence, revolving round its centre of gravity, is contained with itself like a couplet, and each paragraph forms itself into a stanza'),[35] can be seen on the one hand as a sort of trademark or brandname, a stubbornly idiosyncratic attempt to preserve 'personality' in an era of increasingly anonymous, commodified literary production. On the other hand, however, that style can be read as a turning inward and away, on the part of the literary intellectual, from the pressing business of material life, which throughout Johnson's gloomy *oeuvre* figures as irritant and distraction rather than as vitalizing bustle. The eccentricity of Johnson's writing is that of a resoundingly public discourse which is nevertheless profoundly self-involved; it marks a thickening of language in which words, as Hazlitt sees, become objects in their own right, and so suggest a certain social dislocation in contrast to the lucid transparency of the earlier periodicalists. Johnson is both grandly generalizing sage and 'proletarianized' hack; and it is the dialectical relation between these incongruous aspects of his work which is most striking. The social alienations of the latter can be found in displaced form in the involuted meditations of the former; and not only in displaced form, for one of Johnson's recurrent motifs is precisely the hazards and frustrations of authorship in a literary mode of production ruled by the commodity. Stripped of material security, the hack critic compensates for and avenges such ignominy in the sententious authority of his flamboyantly individualist style. Moralistic, melancholic and metaphysical, Johnson's writing addresses itself to the social world (he had, Boswell reports, 'a great deference for the general opinion') in the very moment of spurning it; he is, as Leslie Stephen notes, the moralist who 'looks indeed at actual life, but stands well apart and knows many hours of melancholy.'[36] The sage has not yet been driven to renounce social reality altogether; but there are in Johnson ominous symptoms, for all his personal sociability, of a growing dissociation between the literary intellectual and the material mode of production he occupies. He is not in this sense as socially acceptable to later critics as are Addison and Steele, precisely because in his 'rough vigour' and 'obstinate realism' he smacks a little too much of that leaden didacticism which such cavalier-loving critics need at all costs to distance. The English love a character, but they love a lord even more, Johnson is 'more of the bear, and Addison more of the gentleman', comments the charmingly cavalier G.S. Marr;[37] and indeed Boswell himself noted that if Addison was more of a 'Companion', his friend was more of a teacher. One can trace in this shift towards moral dogmatism a looseninng and disturbing of that easy amicability set up between the early periodicalist and his readers, as the genial amateurism of an Addison sours into the grousing of the exploited professional. Leslie Stephen, with Smollett's *Critical Review* particularly in mind, writes of the emergence in eighteenth-century England of the professional critic, the rise of a 'new tribunal or literary Star Chamber' in which the interpersonal discourse of coffee-house literati gradually yields ground to the professional critic whose unenviable task is to render an account of all new books.[38] Johnson, described by a modern biographer as a 'superlatively good hack',[39] wrote only for money and considered a man would be a fool to do otherwise. *The Rambler*, with its considerably glummer tone than the earlier periodicals, its loss of a certain effect of spontaneous sociability, was not designed to be widely popular and sold perhaps 400 copies an issue – about the circulation of T.S. Eliot's *Criterion*. On the other hand, *The Rambler* devoted more space to criticism than any previous journal; and one of Johnson's most signal achievements, with the widely selling *Lives of the Poets*, was to popularize for a general reading public a literary criticism previously associated with pedantry and personal abuse. What made such a general appeal possible was in part Johnson's renowned 'common sense': for him, as for Addison and Steele, the act of literary criticism inhabits no autonomous aesthetic sphere but belongs organically with 'general ideology', indissociable from common styles of judgement and experience, bound up with a *Lebenswelt* which precedes and encompasses all specialist disciplinary distinctions. We are still not at a point where we can speak of 'literary criticism' as an isolable technology, though with Johnson we are evolving towards just that rift between literary intellectual and social formation out of which a fully specialist criticism will finally emerge. In the trek from the cultural politics of Addison to the 'words on the page', the *philosophical* moment of Samuel Johnson – a mind still laying 'amateur' claim to evaluate all social experience, but now isolated and abstracted in contrast to the busily empirical Addison – is a significant milestone.

Among the factors responsible for the gradual disintegration of the classical public sphere, two are of particular relevance to the history of English criticism. The first is economic: as capitalist society develops and market forces come increasingly to determine the destiny of literary products, it is no longer possible to assume that 'taste' or 'cultivation' are the fruits of civilized dialogue and reasonable debate. Cultural determinations are now clearly being set from elsewhere – from beyond the frontiers of the public sphere itself, in the laws of commodity production of civil society. The bounded space of the public sphere is aggressively invaded by visibly 'private' commercial and economic interests, fracturing its confident consensualism. The mutation from literary patronage to the laws of the market marks a shift from conditions in which a writer might plausibly view his work as the product of collaborative intercourse with spiritual equals, to a situation in which the 'public' now looms as an anonymous yet implacable force, the object rather than co-subject of the writer's art. The second reason for the decline of the

public sphere is a political one. Like all ideological formations, the bourgeois public sphere thrives on a necessary blindness to its own perimeters. Its space is potentially infinite, able to incorporate the whole of the
'polite'; no significant interest lies beyond its reach, for
the very criteria of what is to count as a significant
interest lie in its monopolistic possession. The nation –
society as a whole – is effectively identical with the
ruling class; only those wielding a title to speak
rationally, and thus only the propertied, are in a true
sense members of society. 'The gentleman,' as John
Barrell has argued, 'was believed to be the only member
of society who spoke a language universally intelligible;
his usage was 'common', in the sense of being neither a
local dialect nor infected by the terms of any particular
art.'[40] The language of the common people, by contrast,
cannot truly be said to belong to the 'common language':
'Of the laborious and mercantile Part of the People,'
Johnson writes in the *Preface* to his Dictionary, 'the
Diction is in a great Measure casual and mutable . . .
this fugitive Cant, which is always in a State of Increase
or Decay, cannot be regarded as any Part of the durable
Materials of a Language, and therefore must be suffered
to perish with other things unworthy of Preservation.'
Just as the common people are therefore, as Barrell points
out, 'no part of the true language community', so they
form no true part of the political community either. The
interests of the propertied classes are in a real sense all
that politically exists; the boundaries of the public
sphere are not boundaries at all, for beyond them, as
beyond the curvature of cosmic space, there is nothing.

What such a realm will then be unable to withstand is
the inruption into it of social and political interests in
palpable conflict with its own 'universal' rational norms.
Such interests cannot in one sense be recognised as

such, since they fall outside the public sphere's own definitive discourse; but they cannot merely be dismissed either, since they pose a real material threat to that sphere's continuing existence. Habermas dates such a moment in England from the rise of Chartism, as he identifies it in France with the February revolution of 1848; but in the case of England at least, this pinpointing is surely somewhat belated. For what is emerging in the England of the late-eighteenth and early-nineteenth centuries, in that whole epoch of intensive class struggle charted in E.P. Thompson's *The Making of the English Working Class*, is already nothing less than a 'counter-public sphere'. In the Corresponding Societies, the radical press, Owenism, Cobbett's *Political Register* and Paine's *Rights of Man*, feminism and the dissenting churches, a whole oppositional network of journals, clubs, pamphlets, debates and institutions invades the dominant consensus, threatening to fragment it from within. A commentator of 1793 observed gloomily that the 'lowest of the people can read; and books adapted to the capacity of the lowest of the people, on political and all other subjects, are industriously obtruded on their notice.' The newspapers, he added, 'communicate the debates of opposing parties in the senate; and public measures (even confined to a conclave) are now canvassed in the cottage, the manufactory, and the lowest resorts of *plebeian* carousal. Great changes in the public mind are produced by this diffusion; and such changes must produce public innovation.'[41]

It is interesting in this respect to contrast the tone of the early eighteenth-century periodicals with that of their early nineteenth-century counterparts. What distinguishes, indeed well-nigh immortalizes, the bourgeois periodical press of the latter period is what one commentator has summarized as its 'partisan bias, the vituperation, the dogmatism, the juridical tone, the air of omniscience and finality' with which it conducts its critical business.[42] It is the scurrility and sectarian virulence of the *Edinburgh* and the *Quarterly* which have lingered in the historical memory, in dramatic contrast to the ecumenism of an Addison or Steele. In these vastly influential journals, the space of the public sphere is now much less one of bland consensus than of ferocious contention. Under the pressures of mounting class struggle in society as a whole, the bourgeois public sphere is fissured and warped, wracked with a fury which threatens to strip it of ideological credibility. It is not, of course, that the class struggle in society at large is directly reflected in the internecine antagonisms between the various literary organs; these unseemly wranglings are rather a refraction of those broader conflicts into ruling-class culture, divided as it is over how much political repression of the working class is tolerable without the risk of insurrection. Francis Jeffrey, editor of the Whig *Edinburgh Review*, 'had not the slightest desire to end the predominance of landed property or to institute democracy. He was simply frightened of what would happen if the governmental structure did not yield to popular pressure in order to preserve a society otherwise (he thought) threatened with complete subversion.'[43] Fiercely partisan, the *Edinburgh* soon provoked into countervailing existence the Tory *Quarterly Review*; the *London Magazine* set out to break with the political immoderacy of its competitors, rebuked the adolescent polemics of *Blackwood's Magazine* and found itself embroiled in a quarrel which was to result in its editor, John Scott, being killed in a duel. John and Leigh Hunt, editors of the radical *Examiner*, were imprisoned for an alleged libel of the Prince Regent;[44] *Fraser's Magazine* was an insulting rag crammed with doggerel and brutal burlesque. Sir Roger de Coverley and Sir Andrew Freeport were no longer drinking companions in the same club, but deadly rivals. What distinguishes these polemics from the bellicose exchanges of earlier Whigs and Tories is their class-function: they are at root reactions to a threat to the public sphere itself from organized social interests beyond it.

If criticism had to some degree slipped the economic yoke of its earlier years, when it was often no more than a thinly concealed puff for booksellers' wares, it had done so only to exchange such enthralment for a political one. Criticism was now explicitly, unabashedly political: the journals tended to select for review only those works on which they could loosely peg lengthy ideological pieces, and their literary judgements, buttressed by the authority of anonymity, were rigorously subordinated to their politics. Criticism was still in no full sense the product of literary 'experts': most of the *Edinburgh's* lawyers, political theorists and economists wrote from time to time on literary topics.[45] The *Quarterly* savaged Keats, Hazlitt, Lamb, Shelley, Charlotte Brontë; *Blackwood's* ran a vicious campaign against the 'Cockney school' clustered around the *London Magazine*; Jeffrey of the *Edinburgh*, self-appointed guardian of public taste, denounced the Lake poets as regressive and ridiculous, a threat to traditional social rank and the high seriousness of bourgeois morality. Dismayed by such strife, Leigh Hunt looked back nostalgically to the more sedate years of the early century, proclaiming his desire to criticize others 'in as uncritical a spirit of the old fashion as we can'. 'The truth is,' Hunt lamented, 'that criticism itself, for the most part, is a nuisance and an impertinence: and no good-natured, reflecting men would be critics, if it were not that there are worse.'[46] The periodical essayist, in Hunt's view, is 'a writer who claims a peculiar intimacy with the public'; but the 'age of periodical philosophy' is on the wane, driven out by press advertising and the 'mercantile spirit'. 'Our former periodical politicians . . . wrote to establish their own opinions and to acquire reputation; our present, simply to get money . . .'[47] An edition of the *Spectator* of 1831 entered a plea for the classical public sphere: 'Journalism is nothing but the expression of public opinion. A newspaper that should attempt to dictate, must soon perish.'[48] Such highmindedness had in fact long been overtaken by the fissiparousness of public opinion, the commercialization of literary production and the political imperative to process public consciousness in an age of violent class conflict. Even Leigh Hunt, committed though he believed himself to be to the disinterested pursuit of philosophic truth, uneasily acknowledged the need to write with something less than complete candour: 'the growth of public opinion implies the fostering of it',[49] and such fostering of what is now by implication a partially benighted readership demanded a certain diplomatic delicacy. The critic is ideally the mirror but in fact the lamp: his role is becoming the ultimately untenable one of 'expressing' a public opinion he covertly or flagrantly manipulates.

Criticism, then, has become a locus of political contention rather than a terrain of cultural consensus; and it is in this context that we can perhaps best evaluate the birth of the nineteenth-century 'sage'. What the sage represents, one might claim, is an attempt to rescue criticism and literature from the squalid political infighting which alarmed Leigh Hunt, constituting them instead as transcendental forms of knowledge. The growth of idealist aesthetics in Europe, imported into England by Coleridge and Carlyle, is concomitant with this strategy. From the writings of the later Coleridge, through to Carlyle, Kingsley, Ruskin, Arnold and others, literature is extricated from the arena of *Realpolitik* and elevated to a realm where, in the words of one Victorian commentator, 'all might meet and expatiate in common'.[50] Literature will fulfil its ideological functions most effectively only if it sheds all political instrumentality to become the repository of a common human wisdom beyond the sordidly historical. If the sage is driven by history into transcendental isolation, spurred into prophetic print by his vision of cultural degradation yet stripped of a fit audience for his musings by just the same circumstances, he can nevertheless turn this isolation to ideological advantage, making a moral virtue out of historical necessity. If he can no longer validate his critical judgements by sound public standards, he can always interpret the consequent mysteriousness of such judgements as divine inspiration. Carlyle, sagest of the sages, contributed to *Fraser's Magazine* but considered it 'a chaotic, fermenting dung-hill heap of compost',[51] and dreamt of the day when he would be free to write 'independently'. 'I will not degenerate,' he wrote to his future wife, 'into the wretched thing which calls itself an Author in our Capitals and scribbles for the sake of filthy lucre in the periodicals of the day.'[52] Thackeray, praising Carlyle for his supposed refusal to subordinate critical judgement to political prejudice, 'Pray(ed) God we shall begin ere long to love art for art's sake. It is Carlyle who has worked more than any other to give (art) its independence.'[53] The sage is no longer the co-discoursing equal of his readership, his perceptions tempered by a quick sense of their common opinion; the critic's stance in relation to his audience is now transcendental, his pronouncements dogmatic and self-validating, his posture towards social life chillingly negative. Sundered on the rocks of class struggle, criticism bifurcates into Jeffrey and Carlyle, political lackey and specious prophet. The only available alternative to rampant 'interest', it would seem, is a bogus 'disinterestedness'.

Yet disinterestedness in the Romantic period is not merely bogus. In the hands of a Hazlitt, the 'natural disinterestedness of the human mind' becomes the basis of a radical politics, a critique of egocentric psychology and social practice. The 'sympathetic imagination' of the Romantics is disinterestedness as a revolutionary force, the production of a powerful yet decentred human subject which cannot be formalized within the protocols of rational exchange. In the Romantic era, the depth and span of critique which would be equal to a society wracked by political turmoil is altogether beyond the powers of criticism in its traditional sense. The function of criticism passes accordingly to poetry itself – poetry as, in Arnold's later phrase, a 'criticism of life', art as the most absolute, deep-seated response conceivable to the given social reality. No critique which does not establish such an implacable distance between itself and the social order, which does not launch its utterances from some altogether different place, is likely to escape incorporation; but that powerfully enabling distance is also Romanticism's tragedy, as the imagination joyfully transcends the actual only to consume itself and the world in its own guilt-stricken self-isolation. Criticism in the conventional sense can no longer be a matter of delivering verifiable judgements according to shared public norms, for the act of judgement itself is now tainted with a deeply suspect rationality, and normative assumptions are precisely what the negating force of art seeks to subvert. Criticism must therefore either become the enemy of art, as Jeffrey is of Wordsworth, corner for itself some of the creative energy of poetry itself, or shift to a quasi-philosophical meditation on the nature and consequences of the creative act. The Romantic critic is in effect the poet ontologically justifying his own practice, elaborating its deeper implications, reflecting upon the grounds and consequences of his art. Once literary production itself becomes problematical, criticism can no longer be the mere act of judgement of an assured phenomenon; on the contrary, it is now an active principle in the defending, unfolding and deepening of this uneasy practice of the imagination, the very explicit self-knowledge of art itself. Such quasi-philosophical self-reflection will always be ironic, for if truth is nothing less than poetry, how can any non-poetic discourse hope to capture the reality of which it speaks, ensnared as it is in a rationality—that of social discourse itself—which reaches out for truth but can never be equal to it? The critic, then, is no longer in the first place judge, administrator of collective norms or locus of enlightened rationality; nor is he in the first place cultural strategist or political catalyst, for these functions are also passing over to the side of the artist. He is not primarily a mediator between work and audience, for if the work achieves its effects it does so by an intuitive immediacy which flashes between itself and reader and could only be dissipated by passing through the relay of critical discourse. And if the work does not succeed, then it is because there is in truth no fit audience to receive it, because the poet is a nightingale singing in the dark, and thus once again no place for a mediator. If such an audience must be actively constructed, then according to Wordsworth's *Supplementary Essay* of 1815 it is the poet himself who must be foremost in this task, a task of which the critic is indeed the deadly enemy. The question now confronting criticism is simply this: how is it possible to be a critic at all if art is its own self-grounded, self-validating truth, if social discourse is irremediably alienated, and if there is no audience to address in the first place? With the decline of literary patronage and the classical public sphere, the abandonment of literature to the market and the anonymous urbanization of society, the poet or sage is deprived of a known audience, a community of familiar co-subjects; and this severance from any permanent particular readership, which the sway of commodity production has forced upon him, can then be converted to the illusion of a transcendental autonomy which speaks not idiomatically but universally, not in class accents but in human tones, which turns scornfully from an actual 'mass' public and addresses itself instead to the People, to the future, to some potential mass political movement, to the Poetic Genius buried in every breast, to a community of transcendental subjects spectrally inscribed within the given social order. 'Rational' criticism can find no hold here, for it evolved, as we have seen, in response to one form of (political) absolutism, and finds itself equally at a loss when confronted with another form of self-grounded absolutism in the realm of transcendental spirit.

III

The nineteenth century was to produce a category which yoked sage and critical hack uneasily together: 'man of letters'. It is an interestingly elusive term, broader and more nebulous than 'creative writer', not quite synonymous with scholar, critic or journalist. T.W. Heyck has argued that it is the nearest term we have in nineteenth-century England to the significantly absent category of 'intellectual', which was not to gain currency in its modern sense until the 1870s.[54] Like the eighteenth-century periodicalists, the man of letters is the bearer and dispenser of a generalized ideological wisdom rather than the exponent of a specialist intellectual skill, one whose synoptic vision, undimmed by any narrowly technical interest, is able to survey the whole cultural and intellectual landscape of his age. Such comprehensive authority links the man of letters on one side with the sage; but whereas the sage's synopticism is a function of transcendental detachment, the man of letters sees as widely as he does because material necessity compels him to be a *bricoleur*, dilettante, jack-of-all-trades, deeply embroiled for survival in the very commercial literary world from which Carlyle beat his disdainful retreat. The man of letters knows as much as he does because he cannot make a living out of only one intellectual specialism. The expansion of the reading public by the mid-nineteenth century, and consequently of the periodical market, greatly enhanced opportunities of professional writing; G.H. Lewes correctly considered that the possibility of authorship as a profession was due to the periodical press. The man of letters is in this sense a hack; but he is a figure of sagelike ideological authority too, and in the Victorian period one can observe this unsettling coexistence as often as not within the same individuals.

It was a conflict which Thomas Carlyle hoped to resolve by elevating the man of letters to heroic stature, in a gesture which can only seem to us profoundly bathetic. In 'The Hero as Man of Letters', Carlyle writes of the power of print in spreading the word of parliament ('Literature is our Parliament too') and of the press as having superseded both pulpit and senate.[55] Printing brings with it (indeed, Carlyle implies, actually causes) democracy, creating a community of the literate – 'men of letters' – with, so we are informed, incalculable influence. The whole essay, that is to say, represents a strained, nostalgic reinvention of the classical bourgeois public sphere, lauding the power of discourse to influence political life and raising parliamentary reporters to the status of prophets, priests and kings. Yet there is anxiety and ambiguity too: if men of letters are so incalculably influential, why, Carlyle has the realism to ask himself, do they go so dismally unrecognized? The predictably Carlylean response is that the 'Literary Class' is 'disorganic', socially diffuse and disorganized, something less than Guild-like in its corporate social being. No doubt there is an echo here of the later Coleridge's fear of a rootless, déclassé, disaffected caste of intellectuals, which he believed had done much to bring about the French revolution. The unspoken contradiction in

Carlyle's effusion – are men of letters saviours of society or unheeded hacks? – is familiarly Romantic: the poet as unacknowledged legislator, a *dream* of power continually crossed with what purports to be a description of the actual. Does the classical public sphere still exist, or has it disintegrated?

If the sage's judgements are aloofly authoritarian, the man of letters, attached to one or more of the great Victorian periodicals, is still striving to weld together a public sphere of enlightened bourgeois discourse. His role, like that of Addison and Steele, is to be commentator, informer, mediator, interpreter, popularizer; like his eighteenth-century predecessors he must reflect as well as consolidate public opinion, working in close touch with the broad habits and prejudices of the middle-class reading public. 'The ability to assimilate and interpret,' as Heyck puts it, 'rated as a higher quality than the ability to report special knowledge.'[56] To the extent that the Victorian man of letters achieved considerable success in this task, the bourgeois public sphere may be said to have survived in some form into the mid-nineteenth century. Heyck points out that, given the small size of the electorate before 1867 and its essentially middle-class composition, it is probable that any important novel, historical work or social polemic would have reached 'a very large proportion of the governing elite'. 'Through their newspapers, periodicals and books,' he adds, 'the men of letters wrote directly for all the people who counted in decision-making.'[57] Many of them in addition had close personal and familial relations with men of affairs and the ruling class. Sharing common standards with their audience, they could write out of an instinctive sense of what would be popular, intelligible and acceptable. Leslie Stephen believed that the man of letters had to 'develop a living literature by becoming a representative of the ideas which really interested the whole cultivated classes, instead of writing merely for the exquisite critic.'[58] In an essay on 'The First Edinburgh Reviewers', he winced at a brutally dismissive judgement of Jeffrey's on *Wilhelm Meister*, precisely because it suggested a critic damagingly estranged from a sense of his audience's common sensibilities. 'There is a kind of indecency, a wanton disregard of the general consensus of opinion, in such treatment of a contemporary classic . . . which one would hope to be now impossible.'[59]

The critic's dilemma, as Peter Hohendahl phrases it, is whether to make his judgements on behalf of the broad public or of the minority; and the answer for the Victorian man of letters is not quite so straightforward as Stephen's faith in public consensus would seem to suggest. For the Victorian intellectual climate is one of deep ideological turmoil and insecurity; and in such a situation the man of letters cannot be an exactly equal partner in the dialogue with his audience. His task is to instruct, consolidate and console – to provide a disturbed, ideologically disorientated readership with the kind of popularizing summaries of contemporary thought, all the way from geological discoveries to the Higher Criticism, which might stem the socially disruptive tides of intellectual bemusement. The man of letters, as Heyck argues, 'was expected to help the audience through the troubles of economic, social and religious change';[60] his function was to explain and regulate such change as much as to reflect it, thus rendering it less ideologically fearful. He must actively reinvent a public sphere fractured by class struggle, the internal rupturing of bourgeois ideology, the growth of a confused, amorphous reading public hungry for information and consolation, the continued subversion of 'polite' opinion by the commercial market, and the apparently uncontrollable explosion and fragmentation of knowledges consequent upon the accelerating division of intellectual labour. His relation to his audience, that is to say, must be one of subject to object as well as in some sense subject to subject; a nervous responsiveness to public opinion must find its place within a didactic, covertly propagandist posture towards his readership, processing knowledge in the act of providing it.

In this sense the man of letters is contradictorily located between the authoritarianism of the sage and the consensualism of the eighteenth-century periodicalists, and the strains of this dual stance are obvious enough. Jeffrey was already complaining in the *Edinburgh* that 'it is really provoking to find how very slowly truth and sound reason make their way, even among the reading classes of the community';[61] and the problem finds interesting formulation in Walter Bagehot's essay of 1855 on 'The First Edinburgh Reviewers':

It is indeed a peculiarity of our times, that we must instruct so many persons. On politics, on religion, on all less important topics still more, every one thinks himself competent to think – in some casual manner does think – to the best of our means must be taught to think – rightly. Even if we had a profound and far-reaching statesman, his deep ideas and long-reaching vision would be useless to us, unless we could impart a confidence in them to the mass of influential persons, to the unelected Commons, the unchosen Council who assist at the deliberations of the nation. In religion now the appeal is not to the technicalities of scholars, or the fiction of reclusive schoolmen, but to the deep feelings, the sure sentiments, the painful strivings of all who think and hope. And this appeal to the many necessarily brings with it a consequence. We must speak to the many so that they will listen – that they will like to listen –

that they will understand. It is of no use addressing them with the forms of science, or the rigour of accuracy, or the tedium of exhaustive discussion. The multitude are impatient of system, desirous of brevity, puzzled by formality.[62]

What provides such instruction, Bagehot goes on to add, is 'the review-like essay and the essay-like review'. What he is fearing and regretting here is the decline of the bourgeois public sphere – the 'unelected Commons . . . who assist at the deliberations of the nation' – in an epoch of shallow understanding and opinionated individualism, where the 'unchosen Council' has spread beyond the reliably enlightened to encompass an amorphous, variably educated, culturally philistine middle class. In one sense such people are still on a par with the author himself – 'influential persons' who at least in some casual manner think rightly. But they are also, in a crucial Victorian term, a *mass* of influential persons, and within a few lines have degenerated to a 'multitude'. If they casually think rightly, they must nonetheless be taught to think rightly: 'The modern man must be told what to think,' Bagehot remarks later in the same essay, 'shortly, no doubt, but he *must* be told it.' The political anxiety behind the italicization is palpable. The middle-class readership is now less the critic's collaborative equal in the enterprise of cultural enlightenment than an anonymous object whose sentiments and opinions are to be moulded by techniques of intellectual simplification. An 'amateur' eschewal of technical discourse is now less (as with Addison) part of the very nature of true knowledge than a tactical ploy in the diffusion of it. An ideal of the classical public sphere is still acknowledged, but the political urgency of its reconstitution imparts to the critic's own language a dogmatic insistence potentially at odds with that ideal itself. It is not clear whether it is imperative to disseminate the *ideas* of the putative far-seeing statesman, or merely to generate pervasive emotional confidence in them; are the middle-class masses to be given intellectual illumination, or merely to be enkindled and reassured? Bagehot treats the 'influential persons' of the middle class as though they were the *working* class: intemperate, thickheaded, swayed by emotion, incapable of thought other than in its most untaxing economical forms. The classical public sphere is certainly in disarray, and with it the role of the critic. The man of letters must be at once source of sagelike authority and canny popularizer, member of a spiritual clerisy but plausible intellectual salesman. John Morley, editor of the *Fortnightly Review*, speaks of his contributors as being entrusted with the 'momentous task of forming public opinion',[63] and while the declared goal is traditional to the public sphere, that 'momentous' tells its own bleak story. The critic is now both inside and outside the public arena, responding attentively from within only the more effectively to manage and mould opinion from some superior external vantage-point. It is a posture which threatens to invert the priorities of correction and collaboration evident in the *Tatler* and *Spectator*, where the former was possible and tolerable only on the basis of the latter.

The cultural unevenness of the nineteenth-century reading public is important in this respect. In the epoch of Addison and Steele, the frontiers between 'polite society' and the rest of the nation were rigorous and palpable. There were, naturally, many degrees of literacy in eighteenth-century England; but there was an obvious distinction between those who could 'read', in a sense of the term inseparable from ideological notions of gentility, and those who could not. The nineteenth-century man of letters must suffer the blurring and troubling of this reasonably precise boundary. What is now most problematical is not illiteracy, which is after all a sort of absolute, determinable condition, but those who, while well able to read, are not quite able to 'read' – those who, capable of reading in a physiological and psychological but not culturally valorized sense, threaten to deconstruct the fixed opposition between 'influential persons' and 'multitude'. What is most ideologically undermining is a literacy which is not literacy, a form of reading which transgresses the frontier between blindness and insight, a whole nation which reads but not in your sense of reading, and which is therefore neither quite literate nor illiterate, neither firmly within one's categories nor securely the other of them. It is at this deconstructive point, this *aporia* of reading, that the critic finds himself addressing an audience which is and is not his equal. Poised precariously between clerisy and market forces, he represents the last historical attempt to suture these realms together; and when the logic of commodity production will render such strivings obviously utopian, he will duly disappear from historical sight. The twentieth-century man of letters is a more notably 'minority' figure than his Victorian predecessor.

By the mid-nineteenth century, as the passage from Bagehot suggests, the drive to consolidate the bourgeois reading public has become increasingly defensive. Encircled and assailed by alien interests, grievously confused and internally divided as a consequence, the public sphere is now compelled to view its own activities in an ideological light. The provision of social information or moral education can no longer be innocent of a will to class solidarity in the face of grave political danger. Knowledge and power are no longer blandly dissociable; the diffusion of enlightenment can no longer be conceived à la Addison as a delightful end in itself, as the natural self-pleasuring of polite conversation, but is guiltily entwined with the very class issues it ought in principle to transcend. For the eighteenth century, as we have seen, ruling-class interests and rationality were really all there were; and because this problematic was universal, because to speak politely at all was only possible within it, there was less need than there was in the Victorian/era to fear that men and women might not speak 'rightly'. What they said, the particular statements they formed, might well be incorrect, but the act of speaking politely, governed as it was by certain rational protocols, was already a kind of rightness of its own. Once the critic begins to fear that his interlocutors, left to their own devices, might wander off into gross ideological error, he must jettison any trust that the free market of discourse, left to its own workings, will deliver the appropriate moral and intellectual goods. It is no longer possible to believe with Samuel Johnson that 'about those things on which the public thinks long it commonly attains to think right.'[64] The bleak courage of John Stuart Mill's *On Liberty* (1859) is precisely this clenched eleventh-hour faith that the classical public sphere might still be viable – that the free play of opinion, untrammelled by 'sinister interests', will finally produce a richer, more perdurable truth than any centralized regulation of the discursive marketplace. It is a sign of the times, nevertheless, that the concept of 'public opinion' is now, for Mill, resoundingly negative – one of the tyrannical forces which jeopardize, ironically enough, the 'public sphere' itself. He writes of the 'tyranny of the majority', and of 'the ascendancy of public opinion in the state' as a dangerously homogenizing force. 'As the various social eminences which enabled persons entrenched on them to disregard the opinion of the multitude, gradually become levelled; as the very idea of resisting the will of the public, when it is positively known that they have a will, disappears more and more from the minds of practical politicians; there ceases to be any social support for non-conformity – any substantive power in society, which, itself opposed to the ascendancy of numbers, is interested in taking under its protection opinions and tendencies at variance with those of the public.'[65] The principle of the public sphere has been turned against itself with a vengeance: the enlightened discoursing subjects of the ruling class, having been forced to extend the franchise, and with it the boundaries of the public sphere, to the 'multitude', suddenly find themselves an unprotected minority within their own domain – and this before the working class yet has the vote. An earlier Benthamite confidence in the power of public opinion now appears naive: Bentham, Mill writes in his celebrated essay on him, had pointed out 'how exclusively partial and sinister interests are the ruling power (in Europe), with only such check as is imposed by public opinion – which being thus, in the existing order of things, perpetually apparent as a source of good, he was led by natural partiality to exaggerate its intrinsic excellence'.[66] The companion piece to the essay on Bentham is thus the study of Coleridge, whose project for a clerisy of the enlightened might temper the worst effects of a now tyrannical public sphere. *On Liberty*, however, deploys a trust in the principle of that sphere against the depressing reality of it. To trust the free play of discourse in such conditions is of course to take an enormous risk; but Mill is well aware that error, ideological turmoil and political vulnerability may be the price one has to pay if the deep discursive structures of the bourgeois subject – freedom, equality, autonomy, reciprocity – are to be preserved at all. Matthew Arnold, characteristically, is unwilling to pay any such price: force till right is ready, state repression in the name of individual liberty, are with him the slogans of a liberalism which, observing the final disintegration of the public sphere, shifts steadily towards autocracy. Arnold is prepared to sacrifice the politico-discursive forms of classical bourgeois society for the sake of its social content; Mill is much less convinced that truths produced from beyond the spontaneous exchanges of the public sphere are as valuable as the formal truths which such exchanges embody.

If the task of the man of letters is to assess each strain of fresh specialist knowledge by the touchstone of a general humanism, it is gradually becoming clear that such an enterprise cannot withstand the proliferating division of intellectual labour in English society. G.H. Lewes, editor of *The Leader* and, before Morley, of *The Fortnightly*, seemed more than any of his *confrères* to unite the whole range of cultural activities in his own person, as actor, theatre critic, amateur scientist, journalist, philospher and penner of pot-boiling farces; but this very eclecticism was a source of anxiety rather than satisfaction to him. 'How few men of letters *think* at all!' he once complained.[67] Will Ladislaw's attractively varied talents, energizing enough in 1832, were acquiring more than a smack of dilettantism by the time of *Middlemarch*'s publiccation. The general 'amateur' humanism of the man of letters could less and less provide a plausible centre of coherence for the conflictual discursive formation of late Victorian England. Such humanism, with its trust in ethical responsibility, individual autonomy and the transcendentally free self, was coming under severe assault by some of the very intellectual developments it attempted to process and defuse. Newman made a final, doomed attempt to re-establish theology in its medieval role as metalanguage, queen of sciences and meaning of meanings. Leslie Stephen looked back nostalgically to the previous century, with its apparently more homogeneous literary culture. That homogeneity, he believed, was already under pressure by the time of Johnson, though even at that point English society was 'still small enough to have in the club a single representative body and one man (Johnson) as dictator'.[68] In a later epoch, Carlyle and Macaulay, still to some degree representative figures, 'could only be the leaders of a single group or section in the more complex society of their time, though it was not yet so multitudinous and chaotic as the literary class in our own.'[69] If Stephen looks back nostalgically, however, he does so with a certain condescension. Much as he admires Addison, he cannot help finding his ethical, aesthetic and psychological thought superficial, as indeed did Matthew Arnold: 'A man who would speak up on such topics now must be a grave philosopher, who has digested libraries of philosophy.'[70] Addison, in short, is naively unprofessional: with his 'sancta simplicitas' he does not suspect that he is 'going beyond his tether'. The Victorian man of letters may resist specialization for both economic and ideological reasons, but he is impressed and influenced enough by it to patronize eighteenth-century criticism as callow, and perhaps detect in it an unsettling parody of his own growing superfluousness. The problem of the Victorian man of letters is one which has never ceased to dog the English critical institution, and is indeed quite unresolved even today: either criticism strives to justify itself at the bar of public opinion by maintaining a general humanistic responsibility for the culture as a whole, the amateurism of which will prove increasingly incapacitating as bourgeois society develops; or it converts itself into a species of technological expertise, thereby establishing its professional legitimacy at the cost of renouncing any wider social relevance. The later work of Leslie Stephen represents the last lonely moment of the Victorian man of letters, before the full force of this contradiction is unleashed.

In Victorian England, then, the critic as mediator or middleman, shaping, regulating and receiving a common discourse, is at once ideologically imperative and, with the professionalization of knowledges, warring of ideological standpoints and rapid expansion of an unevenly educated reading public, a less and less feasible project. The very conditions which provoke such a role into existence end by defeating its possibility. In other senses, too, the critic's traditional role as mediator was proving redundant. Dickens, for example, required no middleman between himself and his public; the popular authors were themselves assuming one of the critic's functions, moulding and reflecting the sensibility by which they were consumed. The critic cannot defeat the laws of the literary commodity, much as he might quarrel with them. A 'juridical' critical discourse on such writers is still appropriate in the periodicals, measuring how far particular literary products violate or conform to certain aesthetic-ideological norms; but this discourse must be conducted at a distance from the market, and it is the market, not the critical discourse, which has the upper hand in determining what is acceptable. The place in Victorian society where these two apparatuses – commercial and juridical – most powerfully intersect is in the twin figures whom one might well term the period's most important literary critics: Charles Mudie and W.H. Smith. The censorious, moralistic owners of the two major circulating libraries, Mudie and Smith effectively monopolized Victorian literary production, determining both the form and character of what was actually written. Both men actively intervened in the selection of books for their libraries, and regarded themselves as the protectors of public morality.[71] In the face of such massively concentrated economic and cultural power, no classical public sphere was remotely conceivable.

There was another reason for the critic's growing redundancy. For if criticism's task was more moral than intellectual, a matter of guiding, uplifting and consoling a dispirited middle class, what could more effectively fulfil these ends than literature itself? 'Morals and manners,' remarked Thackeray, 'we believe to be the novelist's best themes; and hence prefer romances which do not treat of algebra, religion, political economy, or any other abstract science.'[72] The most searching, invigorating social critic was the writer himself; for all those who turned to Walter Bagehot for spiritual solace, there were a great many more who opened *Adam Bede* or *In Memoriam*. Once criticism had identified one of its major tasks as ideological reassurance, it was in danger of arguing itself out of a job – for this was precisely what literature itself was, among other things, designed to provide. George Eliot's contributions to the *Westminster Review* are those of a distinguished woman of letters; but the specialist knowledge she occasionally trades in here will only become truly efficacious when fleshed out in fictional form. As woman of letters, Eliot is from time to time partisan spokesperson for minority 'progressive' views; as novelist, she can supposedly transcend such prejudices, gathering them into that many-sided totality that is literary realism. If the middle-class masses, as Bagehot believes, will suffer edification only in graphic, economical, non-systematic form, what better medium of such enlightenment could there be but literature? And where then does that leave the critic?

Critical partisanship is in general less ferocious in mid-century than it had been in the earlier decades; but it still poses an obstacle to the consensual task which criticism must set itself, whether in the militant Utilitarianism of the *Westminster*, the radical free thought of the *Fortnightly* or the Toryism of the *Quarterly*. How was a middle-class readership to be ideologically primed and homogenized when the intellectuals to whom they anxiously turned could be observed publicly scrapping with each other over the most fundamental issues? The *Fortnightly* had tried to break with the rampant sectarianism of the older journals, offering itself as a 'platform for the discussion of all questions by the light of pure reason, on lines agreeable to impartial intellect alone.'[73] Another attempt at 'disinterestedness' arrived with the establishment of the *Saturday Review*, in which criticism strove to sever itself once and for all from the public realm. Run as a hobby by its editor Beresford Hope, the *Saturday* was an organ of Oxford high culture, given to snobbish contempt for such popular authors as Dickens. Its contributors, in the words of its historian, 'assumed a pose of lofty condescension and infallibility which gave their utterances an oracular rather than argumentative tone'.[74] Characterized by a 'dry and ungenerous negativism', the *Saturday* poured scorn upon popular taste and the mass literary market; it reverted to an 'eighteenth-century aristocratic attitude towards literary men', regretting the growth of a professional layer of writers with no significant role in the sphere of public affairs. It was a prime example of that 'higher journalism' which, as Christopher Kent has argued, provided 'an ideal medium of cultural authority ready to serve the newly awakened ambitions of the universities'.[75] At the turn of the century journalism had been in low repute, and

Jeffrey had hesitated before accepting the editorial chair of the *Edinburgh;* later on, as Kent comments, 'journalism was one of the obvious means by which the universities might speak to the nation.'[76] What they told the nation, however, was for the most part insolently reproving; in this sense the pulling of some periodical journalism into the orbit of an aloof, socially alienated academia represents another stage in the dissolution of the classical public sphere. The 'higher journalism' signifies less a renewal of that sphere, than a partial annexation of it by a sullenly anti-social criticism.

The *Saturday*'s dignified retreat to traditionalist culture in the face of mass literature and the professional writer was one drastic response to the crisis of Victorian criticism. Like the role of the man of letters, however, it was a strategy doomed to failure. The dilemma of Victorian criticism is that the two paths open to it – roughly speaking, those of hack and sage – were both *cul-de-sacs*. The man of letters, as we have seen, is on the point of being overtaken by intellectual specialization and the unpalatable truth that the public taste he seeks to form is now decisively determined by the market. The sage, partly in reaction to this dismal condition, removes himself from the social arena to less contaminated heights, but in doing so merely lapses into ineffectual idealism. This is nowhere more graphically illustrated than in the work of Matthew Arnold. If the *Saturday* viewed itself, deludedly enough, as disinterested, it was still not disinterested enough for Arnold, who considered its tone too assertive, its views too provincial, for it to serve as a true bastion of unbiased intelligence.[77] Arnold himself desires a criticism so supremely objective and non-partisan that it will transcend all particular social classes and interests, seeing the object as it really is. For this purpose, criticism must steadfastly refuse to enter upon the realm of social practice, which is quite distinct from the sphere of ideas; it must seek to establish what is best in human thought 'irrespectively of practice, politics, and everything of the kind'.[78] The politicization of criticism in the sectarian polemics of the journals is an obstacle to the free play of the mind; criticism, accordingly, must withdraw – for a while, at least – into the academic sphere, encircled as it is by a society incapable of fine discrimination. From this serene vantage-point it will equally survey all interests, innocent of any tendentiousness itself beyond the will to truth; but the more capaciously universal its discourse thus becomes ('perfection', 'sweetness and light', 'the best that has been thought and said'), the more it will lapse into utter vacuousness. Criticism, or Culture, will be able to address itself to every sector of social experience only by a *kenosis* so complete that it loses all definitive identity and thus addresses each sector with absolutely nothing to say. Its identity will be entirely negative: whatever is the other of any specific social interest. Its superiority and invulnerability as a (non-) concept will thus be in direct proportion to its impotence. Culture is the negation of all particular claims in the name of the totality – a totality which is therefore purely void because it is no more than a totalization of negated moments. In order to preserve its effectiveness, criticism must divorce itself so radically from the region into which it intervenes that it consumes itself in its own luminous purity and so has no effectiveness whatsoever. The purity of its disinterestedness is the blankness of a cypher; only by a drastic estrangement from social life can it hope to engage fruitfully with it. Culture, like God or the oriental *neti neti* (not this, nor that), is at once everywhere and nowhere – that which, transcendent of all articulate interests, is ineffable and without extension, discernible only in the mournful resonance of the celebrated 'touch-stones', a rich interiority of life which finally eludes discourse altogether.

Yet at the same time culture, or criticism, cannot be this at all. Culture, once confronted with anarchy, must be no mere pious abstraction but a strenuous social force, a programme of social practice and educational reform, a transformative project which will weld the East End into unity with Whitehall. For Arnold as much as for Addison and Steele, criticism is directed towards class solidarity, the creation of a society of enlightened equals. The critic, as Walter Benjamin put it, is a 'strategist in the literary battle',[79] and Arnold, through the apparatus of state schools, wishes urgently to re-invent for the nineteenth century that osmosis of bourgeois and aristocratic values to which the early eighteenth-century periodicals had also dedicated their energy. Leslie Stephen refers to Addison as 'a genuine prophet of what we now call Culture',[80] reading back this allusive Arnoldian term into the earlier period; but though for both writers culture involves class solidarity, the fact that Arnold is dealing with social classes whose interests are historically irreconcilable drives his notion of culture into a transcendentalism quite foreign to the *Spectator*. The vital difference, at this later stage of bourgeois society, is that cultural collaboration within the hegemonic social bloc has become neurotically defensive: its major aim is to incorporate an unruly proletariat, as Arnold makes sufficiently clear:

> It is itself a serious calamity for a nation that its tone of feeling and grandeur of spirit should be lowered or dulled. But the calamity appears far more serious still when we consider that the middle classes, remaining as they are now, with their narrow, harsh, unintelligent, and unattrac-

tive spirit and culture, will almost certainly fail to mould or assimilate the masses below them, whose sympathies are at the present moment actually wider and more liberal than theirs. They arrive, these masses, eager to enter into possession of the world, to gain a more vivid sense of their own life and activity. In this their irrepressible development, their natural educators and initiators are those immediately above them, the middle classes. If these classes cannot win their sympathy or give them their direction, society is in danger of falling into anarchy.[81]

For Arnold, unlike Addison and Steele, there now exist organized interests beyond the bourgeois sphere; and the drive to consolidate that sphere is inseparable from the will to break and integrate them. Culture must be 'classless', and 'the men of Culture the true apostles of equality', because the proletariat now exists; and the language of criticism must be ill-defined enough to encompass them. Ruling-class values must be modulated into metaphors open-textured enough to conceal their class-roots and take effect as much in the East End as in the West. It is the very urgency of the political situation which forces Arnold into his vague poeticism, the depth of his anxiety which breeds his apparent blandness. The Populace are an alien class who must but cannot be incorporated into civilized discourse; accordingly, Arnold must either stretch that discourse to the point where it purges itself of all class idiom but, along with it, of all political substance, or speak a more identifiable class-language which is sharp and substantial only at the price of potentially alienating the Populace. It is clear in any case that criticism still has no alternative between a disreputable collusion in class interests and a bankrupt 'transcendence' of them; it is not for nothing that the Arnold of the poetry is always either suffocating among city crowds or stifling for lack of air on a mountain top.[82]

Criticism, he believes, must be 'urbane' rather than ponderously moralistic; but this urbanity is far removed from the metropolitan bustle which fascinated Addison and Steele. Arnold desires to re-create the bland tones of such writing in divorce from its material basis, carry culture into the East End while simultaneously ensconcing it in the academies. An academy of the French kind, were it possible in England, would establish a 'force of educated opinion';[83] the classical public sphere might be reinvented in the form of a clerisy, which would then doubtless radiate its influence into society as a whole. Yet the ideologies of public sphere and clerisy are in fact at odds: the clerisy, from Coleridge onwards, arises on the ruins of the classical public sphere, as a 'vertical' reorganizing of that sphere's 'horizontal' power relations. Arnold's academy is not the public sphere, but a means of defence against the actual Victorian public. His appeals for state intervention in questions of culture – to the state as embodiment of right reason – reflect the passing of the classical liberal capitalist economy, as the state begins to reach far into the sphere of commodity exchange in the economically depressed closing decades of the nineteenth century. Such state intervention, as Habermas argues, is fatal to the classical public sphere, which thrived precisely upon a separation between the state and civil society. With the modern 'statification' of society and socialization of the state, with the transgression of traditional boundaries between private and public, the space of the classical public sphere rapidly dwindles.

Criticism, then, has the unwelcome choice of preserving a political content, thus gaining in social relevance what it loses in a partiality disruptive of the very public sphere it seeks to construct; or of assuming a transcendental standpoint beyond that sphere, thus safeguarding its integrity at the price of social marginality and intellectual nullity. The man of letters represents an awkward hesitation between these options. What actually happened in the course of the nineteenth century was that criticism entered those institutions to which Arnold had looked for the harmonious culture lacking in the periodicals: the universities. I have argued elsewhere that the constitution of 'English literature' as an academic subject in Victorian England fulfilled a number of ideological purposes. 'English' was, among other things, a project designed to pacify and incorporate the proletariat, generate sympathetic solidarity between the social classes, and construct a national cultural heritage which might serve to undergird ruling-class hegemony in a period of social instability.[84] In this sense, the emergence of 'English' brought to fruition the enterprise of the sages, establishing literature as a transcendental object of enquiry. But the founding of English as a university 'discipline' also entailed a professionalization of literary studies which was quite alien to the sage's 'amateur' outlook, and more resolutely specialist than the man of letters could afford to be. The man of letters was, so to speak, an academic without a university, an 'extra-mural' scholar responsive to the demands of the public world. The academicization of criticism provided it with an institutional basis and professional structure; but by the same token it signalled its final sequestration from the public realm. Criticism achieved security by committing political suicide; its moment of academic institutionalization is also the moment of its effective demise as a socially active force. Within academic English, the conflict between 'amateur' and 'professional' was to continue, transposed into a quarrel between 'criticism' and 'scholarship': academic literary scholarship develops apace from the Victorian period onwards as a technical specialism, while academic criticism retains some nebulous preoccupation with 'life' as well as 'letters'. The dispute, however, is for the most part a domestic one, conducted within an institution which permits the critic's voice to be 'disinterested' to the precise extent that it is effectively inaudible to society as a whole.

The final quarter of the nineteenth century witnesses the establishment of the specialized intellectual journal – *Mind, Notes and Queries,* the *English Historical Review* – in which the growing professionalization and compart-mentalization of knowledges is directly reflected. The traditional man of letters, his authority diminished by the universities as centres of specialized research, is also effectively ignored by a mass readership. Intellectual rather than 'intellectual-cum-moral' leadership takes over, as Heyck comments, and the man of letters is despised by late nineteenth-century academics for his shallow eclecticism, partisanship and moral pretensions.[85] Leslie Stephen had been editor of the *Cornhill* magazine, which published such 'high' literary art as Henry James alongside popular romantic fiction; as the journal's readership steadily fell, its middle-brow tastes at odds with Stephen's own intellectual interests, the editorship was taken over by a popular novelist and Stephen turned his attention instead to the *Dictionary of National Biography.* He fell victim, that is to say, to the disintegration of the bourgeois public sphere, squeezed out of existence as it was between university and market, the academicization and commercialization of letters. 'The disintegration of the reading public into the broad masses and the "educated class",' writes Peter Hohendahl, 'prevents the critic from identifying with any general consensus and defining his role in that context.'[86] The *fin-de-siècle* also saw a proliferation of purely 'literary' reviews such as the *Savoy* – precious, exotic, hothouse growths which in their own way marked the dissevering of literature from social concerns. The twentieth century was to see the replacement of the Victorian periodical with the 'little magazine', which as with Eliot's *Criterion* was often enough self-consciously the organ of an elite. It is, ironically, in the modern age that criticism is able to rediscover one of its traditional roles; for the difficulty of the modernist writing associated with such reviews as the *Criterion* and the *Egoist* demands a labour of mediation and interpretation, the shaping of a readerly sensibility to receive such works, as the writing of a Dickens or Trollope did not. That mediation, however, is no longer to a broad middle-class readership, through journals which might exert influence on a majority of the ruling class; it remains more a transaction within academia than one between academy and society.

IV

The contradiction on which criticism finally runs
aground – one between an inchoate amateurism and a
socially marginal professionalism – was inscribed
within it from the outset. John Barrell has shown how in
the eighteenth century such a contradiction can already
be discerned in the idea of the gentleman. The
eighteenth-century gentleman was of no determinate
occupation, and it was precisely this disinterested
detachment from any particular worldly engagement
which allowed him equably to survey the entire social
landscape. The gentleman was custodian of the comprehensive view, representative of a many-sided humanity
which any specialist expertise could only impoverish.
But this very transcendence of the socially particular was
also a kind of limitation – for how could the gentleman
speak authoritatively of that from which he was dissociated? 'If the gentleman,' as Barrell argues, 'is
described as a man of no determinate occupation, it
must seem that any degree of participation on his part in
the affairs of society must compromise him . . . But if he
does nothing, he can learn nothing.'[87] By the mid-
eighteenth century, with a deepening division of labour,
a perception that society is no longer open to comprehensive inspection can be felt at work; Barrell sees

Johnson's periodical essays as embodying a wide range of responses to the recognition that 'society and social knowledge are now so complex that it has become impossible for any individual to understand them as a whole . . . the titles of Johnson's periodicals – the *Idler,* the *Rambler* – suggest something of the rhetorical irony by which Johnson can at once avow and cope with the loss of a general view.'[88] 'There seem,' Johnson writes in *Rambler* 19, 'to be some souls suited to great, and others to little employments; some formed to soar aloft, and take in wide views, and others to grovel on the ground, and confine their regard to a narrow sphere.' Few defter formulations of the misfortunes of the critic could be imagined. Johnson is already glumly aware of the relative ineffectualness of his own 'amateur' moralizing in an increasingly specialist society, as Elizabeth Bruss has noted. 'Because his judgements can still appeal to general principles and common public standards,' she writes, 'there is nothing veiled or mysterious about Johnson's authority and no need for recondite faculties or peculiar expertise to justify his inclusions and exclusions. Indeed, there is a strong sense of public fellowship in Johnson's criticism and an increasingly balanced mode of address that suggests that, as yet, there is little recognized difference between those who write (either poetry or criticism) and those who read. But his outspoken resistance to specialization of any kind, the occasional strenuousness of his efforts to connect moral, psychological, scientific and aesthetic norms, suggests that the balance is extremely precarious and already threatened.'[89]

The balance remained just as precarious in the twentieth century, as the *Scrutiny* movement was to confirm. In his essay on 'Johnson and Augustanism', F.R. Leavis quotes with approval Joseph Krutch's comments on the eighteenth-century art of conversation, which proceeds on the 'assumption that in so far as a subject was discussible at all, it was best discussed in terms of what is generally called (without further definition) "common sense" and that any intelligent and well-educated gentleman, no matter what his special aptitudes might be, was as competent as any other to settle questions philosophical, theological or even scientific'. 'Common sense' Krutch defines as 'the acceptance of certain current assumptions, traditions and standards of value which are never called in question because to question any of them might be to necessitate a revision of government, society and private conduct more thoroughgoing than anyone liked to contemplate'.[90] Leavis endorses this definition, but points out that it suggests 'something far more determinate than "common sense" suggests to us'; he acknowledges Johnson's appeal to the 'common reader', but emphasises that his concern was nevertheless with standards 'above the ordinary level of the ordinary man'. While agreeing with Krutch that Johnson 'did not think of his criticism as something that ought to be essentially different from that general criticism of life which he had made it his business to offer since he first began to write', Leavis nevertheless feels a need to qualify the claim: Johnson (and Krutch) are right to see that there are no 'unique literary values', but 'there *is*, for a critic, a problem of relevance . . . And the ability to be relevant, where works of literary art are concerned, is not a mere matter of good sense; it implies an understanding of the resources of language, the nature of conventions and the possibilities of organization such as can come only from much intensive literary experience accompanied by the habit of analysis.' In failing to recognize this fact, Krutch himself is 'not sufficiently a critic'.[91]

Leavis's ambivalence throughout this essay is understandable. For while he must insist, against technocratic and academicist forms of criticism, that there is no essential discontinuity between literature and social life – that the act of criticism is indissociable from general moral and cultural judgements – he must not do so to the point where he might appear to endorse a cult of genteel amateurism. If the literary critic is merely a sensitive, intelligent judge, what becomes of his 'professional' claim? Criticism cannot be a mere matter of 'good sense', but must engage modes of analysis and forms of specialized experience denied to the 'common reader'. If it is rooted in a common social world, it is also ineluctably set apart from it – just as Johnson himself for Leavis is at once the bearer of an uncommonly rich cultural tradition, comfortably at home within its regulative forms and conventions, yet in his 'robust and racy individuality' something more than a Dryden or a Congreve. The tension between 'amateur' and 'professional', that is to say, merges with a parallel tension within Leavis's thought between sociality and individualism. What he admires in 'Augustanism' is precisely the nourishing presence of a public sphere of which he himself is historically bereft. 'The (Augustan) literary intellectual could feel that in his own grapplings with experience he had society, not merely as ideal tradition, but as a going concern, with him – could feel it in such a way that he didn't need to be conscious of it.'[92] Johnson accordingly occupies a place in his own society which it is not difficult to see Leavis desiring for himself: '(He) is not, like the Romantic poet, the enemy of society, but consciously its representative and its voice, and it is his strength – something inseparable from his greatness – to be so.'[93] Eighteenth-century literary form, Leavis reminds us, is 'intimately associated with Good Form' –

72

but no sooner has he enforced this positive point than its negative corollary strikes him: 'To put it this way is to recall the worst potentialities of Polite Letters – the superficialities and complacencies conjured up by that significant phrase.'[94] Leavis's dilemma is plain: how is he to oppose the literary academics by insisting on the sociality of literature without playing into the hands of the frivolous non-specialism which discerns a bland continuum between Johnson's after-dinner talk and his literary judgements? His attitude to Addison and Steele is significantly ambivalent, blending an appreciation of their sociability with an instinctive dislike of the class tones which accompany it: 'The positive, concentrated and confident civilization we see registered in *The Tatler* and *The Spectator* is impressive, but no profound analysis is necessary to elicit from those bland pages the weaknesses of a culture that makes the Gentleman *qua* Gentleman its criterion, as Queen Anne Augustanism does.'[95] In another essay, Leavis writes with similar ambivalence: 'When Addison says, "a Philosopher, which is what I mean by a Gentleman", he means it. The fruition of life is to be a Gentleman, and no activity is worth pursuing that cannot be exhibited as belonging to that fruition (hence the scorn of the "virtuoso" and the specialist of any kind). The test, the criterion, the significance lies always in the overt social world – the world of common sense, and at the level of polite unspecialized intercourse.'[96] By the end of this sentence, an initially somewhat negative response to the cult of gentility has veered into a more positive approbation of socially rooted criticism. Eighteenth-century culture provokes a conflict in Leavis between the regressive and progressive moments of his petty-bourgeois ideology – between nostaligic admiration for a pre-industrial society which can be seen as homogenous, and an artisanal animus against the cult of gentility which such a society involves. Johnson's moral individualism is thus an essential corrective to those 'debilitating conventionalities, such as forbid the development of the individual sensibility and set up an insulation against any vitalizing recourse to the concrete.'[97] In the figure of Samuel Johnson, a whole range of antinomies in the *Scrutiny* ideology – common reader and professional critic, public sphere and expert elite, civilized intercourse and defensive isolation, cultural convention and independent insight – may be conveniently resolved.

These antinomies reflected the contradictory nature of the *Scrutiny* project. For if it was concerned on the one hand to sustain an 'amateur' liberal humanism, claiming an authoritative title to judge all sectors of social life, it was on the other hand engaged in an internecine struggle to 'professionalize' a disreputably amateur literary academy, establishing criticism as a rigorously analytical discourse beyond the reach of both common reader and common-room wit. In the manner of the eighteenth-century public sphere, it rejected any esoteric aesthetic language and saw both literature and criticism as deeply imbricated with moral and cultural experience as a whole; but the process of defining and discriminating cultural values was now an intensively 'textual' affair, the workings of a specialized, disciplined intelligence which in its focused attentiveness and laboriously achieved insights smacked more of the artisan than the aristocrat. Criticism is more than merely 'literary': in the manner of Addison and Steele it extends its hegemony over politics, philosophy, social thought, everyday life. Yet whereas for Addison and Steele the literary was one more regional sector alongside these, it becomes for *Scrutiny* the central touchstone to which they are to be referred. It is in this way that a generously

'cultural' notion of criticism can be incongruously combined with a narrowly textual one. Toughly 'professional' in critical method, *Scrutiny* also represented the
last-ditch stand of a general ethical humanism in the face
of a society now almost irrecoverably beyond the reach of
such imperatives. The scrupulous empiricism of its
critical techniques ('practical criticism') lent it an
appearance of workmanlike professionalism constantly
undercut by its shoddily imprecise metaphysics (Law-
rentian vitalism).

What *Scrutiny* represented, indeed, was nothing less
than an attempt to reinvent the classical public sphere, at
a time when its material conditions had definitively
passed. Glancing back nostalgically to the days of the
Edinburgh Review, Denys Thompson argued that, if 'our
present plight' was to be mitigated, such an 'intelligent,
educated, morally responsible and politically enlightened public' would have to be recreated.[98] R.G. Cox
praised the shared cultural norms and relatively homogeneous reading public of the 'great reviews', detecting
in them an authority which marked them out as the
'legitimate successors' of Addison and Johnson. Such
reviews, Cox claimed, 'played the major part in creating
for the writers of their age that informed, intelligent and
critical public without which no literature can survive
for very long, and which is so conspicuously lacking
today.'[99] *Scrutiny's* critical ideal was one of civilized,
collaborative exploration: the 'common pursuit of true
judgement', of which the form of Leavis's model critical
proposition – 'This is so, isn't it?' – was offered as exemplary. The reality of *Scrutiny's* historical situation,
however, was exactly the reverse of this: not public
sphere but prophet in the wilderness, not critic as civilized collaborator but critic as unsociable sage. The project, in short, was a contradictory amalgam of the En-

lightenment and Romantic ideologies we have examined, as the disintegration of the actual bourgeois public sphere drove its apologists into a besieged elitism which threatened to destroy that whole ideological model. Collaboration, reasoned enquiry, measured endorsement and dissent could be preserved *within* the *Scrutiny* circle itself, as a frail memory or adumbration of some broader consensus; the group's stance towards the society as a whole, by contrast, was dogmatic, authoritarian and defensive. If Leavis entitled one of his works *The Common Pursuit,* he also inscribed it with a set of epigraphs almost unremittingly negative, dissociated and polemical; if he wished to reinvent the gregarious eighteenth century, he also approved of Henry James's commitment to 'absolutely independent, individual and lonely virtue, and . . . the serenely unsociable (or if need be at a pinch sulky and sullen) practice of the same'. Critical judgement, in the Cambridge tradition of Leslie Stephen, was to be in some sense rationally demonstrable rather than, in Oxford style, mystically ineffable; but this trust in enlightened discourse, once confronted with reasoned opposition, recurrently lapses into the apodicticism of Romantic poet or Victorian sage. The form of Leavis's model critical formulation neatly blends dialogic openness with a certain authoritative insistence confidently anticipating the answer 'yes'.

The attempt to recreate the bourgeois public sphere, in a political society ridden with class-conflict, a culture dominated by the commodity, and an economy which had passed beyond the liberal capitalism which had once made such a sphere possible into its statist and monopolistic stage, was clearly an illusion from the outset. Yet in *Scrutiny* this illusion was compounded with another: for the movement strove to recreate the public sphere *from within the very institutions which had severed criticism from it:* the universities. Criticism was to venture forth from the academies into the lurid regions of advertising and popular culture, but because the values it brought to bear on such phenomena were essentially 'literary', constituted within academia itself, it would always inexorably return there, and in a sense had never, other than in fantasy, ventured out in the first place. *Scrutiny* might challenge the literary canon, but not the constitution of the 'literary' as such, or the university as a 'vital centre'. Its failure to challenge the academic institution sprang from yet another myth: its steadfast belief in an *ideal* university, a spiritual essence of Cambridge quite distinct from the Cambridge which was busy assailing and suppressing its work. In a double mystification, the idealism of *Scrutiny's* hope for a resurgent public sphere was based upon an idealizing of the university, which *was* that public sphere in embryo. That 'English literature' had been academically institutionalized as a displacement of socially engaged criticism rather than as a launching-base for it was a fatal blindspot in the *Scrutiny* case. What seemed a public sphere *in nuce* was in fact an enclave of defensive reaction to the disappearance of the genuine article. *Scrutiny* could hope for a renewed public dialogue between critics, educationalists and other intellectuals, and indeed was reasonably successful in securing it. But such a discursive public realm, unlike the coffee-house community of eighteenth-century England, could be in no way grounded in the political structures of the society as a whole. Leavis and his colleagues were remote enough from the levers of academic power, let alone the political and economic ones; and Leavis himself was conscious enough of this dilemma to write at an early point in his career that 'a consciousness maintained by an insulated minority and without effect upon the powers that rule the world has lost its function.'[100]

Marooned between a hostile academia and a dream of the public sphere, *Scrutiny* was, as Francis Mulhern has termed it, 'meta-political: its role was to invigilate the political domain in the name of "the human", without entering it in its own right.' It attempted, that is, to negotiate the contradiction we have already examined in the critical institution, between an unpalatable partisanship and a sterile dissociation. The journal, as Mulhern points out, represented 'an intellectual formation of a type virtually unknown in and deeply alien to English bourgeois culture: an "intelligentsia" in the classic sense of the term, a body of intellectuals dissociated from every established social interest, pointed in its subordination of amenity to principle, united only by its chosen cultural commitments.'[101] As a historically dispossessed petty-bourgeois intelligentsia, divorced from cultural or political power by the decline of the public sphere within which they might at one period have found a home, the Scrutineers were at liberty to press the claims of (in Leavis's words) a 'free, unspecialized, general intelligence', in the high tradition of the eighteenth-century 'amateur' critic and the Victorian man of letters. Yet the unspecialized general intelligence of a Steele or Addison had never, of course, been 'free'; on the contrary, it was always deeply invested in specific cultural and political interests. It was just that these interests could be viewed as co-extensive with the public sphere as a whole, and so in no sense idiosyncratic or sectarian. Once criticism is forced on to the defensive with the decline of the public sphere, its 'free, unspecialized, general intelligence' is bound to enter into contradiction with the dissentient passion and polemical energy with which it lambasts those social forces responsible for its own effective impotence. In this light, *Scrutiny* emerges as a cross between the *Edinburgh* and the *Saturday*, blending the ferocious lampoons of the former with the high-minded disinterestedness of the latter. At once notional public sphere and partisan minority, spiritual centre and prophetic periphery, *Scrutiny* brought into contradictory unity some of the historical trends of criticism we have investigated, and in doing so marked an impasse beyond which liberal humanism is still unable to move.

'When the general public is considered to have an inadequate aesthetic sense,' writes Peter Hohendahl, 'and only the minority is viewed as a deserving partner for discourse, the general validity of literary criticism can no longer be legitimated by the literary public sphere.'[102] This, in brief, was the dilemma of *Scrutiny*, which wished contradictorily to recreate a public sphere in the conviction that only a minority was capable of true discrimination. At times the minority is seen as the vanguard of a broader public sphere which it will bring into being; at other times minority and public sphere are effectively coterminous. The 'powerlessness' of the classical public sphere, where reason and not force is the norm, is crossed with the powerlessness of the disinherited sect. The 'disinterested' rationality of the classical public sphere, has its basis in the autonomy conferred upon culture by the process of early capitalist commodification: it is only when culture is released from its courtly or ecclesiastical functions to become generally available through the market that it can generate a critical discourse which is 'universal', concerned not only with the immediate social use-value of artefacts but with their abstract truth and beauty. The abstract rules and categories of the Enlightenment are in this sense homologous with the abstract exchange-values of mercantilism. Once the cultural commodity addresses itself indifferently to everybody, the act of criticism apparently sheds its 'interested' character and becomes impersonal; the disinterestedness at the core of the critical act is in this sense the counter-part of the promiscuity of the commodity itself, which has no privileged partner but disports itself with all-comers. The 'disinterestedness' of an Arnold or a Leavis, by contrast, is the product of a later stage of cultural commodification, where the capitalist culture industry has effectively eroded the whole concept of an autonomous art. As Habermas argues: 'When the laws of the market which govern the sphere of commodity exchange and social labour also penetrate the sphere reserved for private people as public, *Räsonnement* (critical judgement) transforms itself tendentially into consumption, and the context of public communication breaks down into acts which are uniformly characterized by individualized reception.'[103] The very material conditions which bring modern criticism into existence, in short, are the conditions which, in developed form, will spell its demise. Once the 'public' has become the 'masses', subject to the manipulations of a commercialized culture, and 'public opinion' has degenerated into 'public relations', the classical public sphere must disintegrate, leaving in its wake a deracinated cultural intelligentsia whose plea for 'disinterestedness' is a dismissal of the public rather than an act of solidarity with them. As long as culture is seen as autonomous of material interests – a situation which, paradoxically, is made possible by the growth of commodity exchange – conflicts of particular cultural interests may be contained and resolved within this overall framework. But as soon as those cultural interests are seen to be dominated and determined by powerful economic forces, or when culture is extended to those with actual or potential interests which fall outside the boundaries of the bourgeois public sphere, that sphere, and the supposed autonomy of art, are simultaneously undermined. Leavis's early writings – *Culture and Environment, Mass Civilization and Minority Culture* – mark this moment of melancholic recognition; and *Scrutiny's* drive to 'professionalize' criticism can be interpreted at once as an attempt to refine the cognitive instruments which might repair this dire situation, and as a retreat from its most intolerable aspects into the closed discourse of a coterie.

The contradictions of such 'professionalization', however, were grievous. For if it helped to lend criticism a legitimacy of which it was now deprived, the very conditions which rendered such a move necessary also prevented its possibility. Criticism needed such legitimacy because of the collapse of the public sphere which had previously validated it; but without such a common set of beliefs and norms, there was really no authority which criticism could legitimate itself *to*. Its discourse was accordingly forced to be self-generating and self-sustaining at the very moment that it offered itself as in some sense rationally demonstrable, circling back upon its own intuitionist ground in the act of addressing a public interlocutor. Leavis's conception of critical practice as occupying a 'third realm', between the brute positivism of the scientific laboratory on the one hand and the vagaries of subjectivism on the other, is significant in this respect: critical judgements must be public, but the 'other' addressed is already in some sense oneself, furnished with one's own intuitive certainties and 'pre-understandings'. This is also true, of course, of the classical public sphere; but whereas Leavis's critical judgements are *in the first place* 'personal', passing in a secondary movement through the relay of a public conversation which leaves them essentially self-identical, the classical public sphere has no such conception of critical response as externalized interiority. On the contrary, publicity is the source and ground of critical judgement, rather than a mere quality of it; in proto-structuralist fashion, the protocols and categories of polite language deconstruct the oppositions between critic as subject, literary object and discursive community. It is this anti-humanism which Leavis fears in 'Augustanism', collusive as it is with the 'automated', impersonal response; his attention shifts accordingly from Addison to Johnson, in whose robust independence he can discern a reflection of his own intractable individualism. But Johnson's independence of judgement, as I have argued, is already in part a function of the loosening of the social relations typical of the classical public sphere; so that the history to which Leavis resorts for mythical resolution of his own troubles is already the pre-history of precisely those dilemmas. There is, nevertheless, a vital difference between Johnson and Leavis in this respect. The dogmatism of both critics may reflect a certain social dissociation, but with Johnson this is still to some degree a matter of style: his judgements, for all their peremptory force, remain rooted in the 'common sense' of which Leavis is notably wary. The intuitive appeals of a Johnson distil the common wisdom of the public sphere, even as their status as laboriously contrived aphorisms betrays an individual self-consciousness no longer altogether at home in that realm. Leavis's intuitionism, by contrast, is ultimately metaphysical in a way Johnson's is not; what speaks in it is 'Life', which at once only ever manifests itself in empirical particulars and is the antagonist of an empiricist 'common sense', the other of public society.

Scrutiny's, 'professionalization' of criticism was at once a reaction against the 'amateur' *bellelettrism* of the literary academics, and a response to the crisis of a liberal humanism whose Arnoldian pieties demanded more precise, particular formulation in the face of the capitalist culture industry. Both of these projects, however, were finally self-defeating. For to 'professionalize' criticism was in a way to rejoin the very academics one opposed, who were, after all, professional state functionaries for all their genteel-amateur ideology; professionalization could in this sense only culminate in reinforcing the very academic institutions of which *Scrutiny* was so correctly critical. 'Practical criticism' may have offered a path to spiritual salvation, but it also offered, more to the point, a way in which criticism might legitimate itself as a valid intellectual 'discipline', thus helping to reproduce the very academic institution which, among other forces, denied 'Life'. As for lending some cutting-edge to liberal humanist pieties, this too proved a potentially self-deconstructing tactic: for to 'professionalize' such a discourse ran the constant risk of destroying the very 'free, unspecialized, general intelligence' which formed its basis. Once more, criticism ran headlong into an impasse between ineffectual generality and rebarbative specialism.

It was *Scrutiny's* signal achievement, however, to manage this incipient contradiction with some aplomb. Indeed there is a sense in which the whole of its programme rested on an implicit denial that the 'technical' and the 'humanist' were in any sense at odds. They were, on the contrary, mutually complementary: the more rigorously criticism interrogated the literary object, the more richly it yielded up that sensuous concreteness and vital enactment of value which were of general human relevance. This belief was the single most powerful 'resolution' of the structural difficulties of criticism which the English critical institution had ever witnessed; and much of *Scrutiny's* immense influence sprang directly from it. A strategy had at last been evolved by which technocrats and gentlemen-scholars, scientism and subjectivism, formalism and frivolity, might be simultaneously outflanked; and for the next few decades no critical movement which did not in some sense found its practice upon this strategy was to achieve major status. I.A. Richards combined a 'scientific' psychology, based upon a neo-Utilitarian calculus of 'appetencies', with a rejection of any autonomously aesthetic realm, an insistence on the continuity between literature and 'life', and an Arnoldian belief in the socially salvific potential of poetry. American New Criticism yoked the sophisticated techniques of minute textual analysis to the task of renewing the delicate textures of human experience, ravaged as they were by industrialism; its tough-minded formalism was at every point coupled with a religious-humanist aesthetic, and the hinge of this coupling was the simultaneously technical and numinous notion of paradox. Northrop Frye, in what appeared for a while an almost unbeatable synthesis, joined the methods of a 'scientific', relentlessly taxonomizing criticism to a religious-humanist vision of literature as the mythical figuration of transcendental desire. Only William Empson, alert in his concept of 'pastoral' to the ironically incongruous play between general humanity and specialized critical intelligence, the suavities of poetic meaning and some more generous, all-encompassing social ambience, seemed to run counter to this most potent of critical orthodoxies.

V

In Richards, Frye and New Criticism, the desirable balance which might have legitimated criticism both within and beyond the academies was not appropriately maintained. Richards's bloodless neo-Benthamism, New Criticism's cloistered aestheticism and Frye's hermetic systematicity had all tipped that balance dangerously in the direction of a critical technocracy which threatened to oust the assorted humanisms (liberal, Christian, conservative) it officially subserved. It was this situation which the social and academic turmoil of the 1960s was starkly to expose. As long as academia maintained its traditional legitimating image, as an institution at once set somewhat apart from society yet of vaguely humanistic relevance to it, criticism was unlikely to be interrogated for its credentials, since this institutional ambiguity matched its own condition exactly. It was at once a somewhat esoteric, self-involved pursuit, as befitted a university discipline, but could at a pinch muster some sort of general case for its socially fruitful effects. In the 1960s, however, the academic institutions, unusually, became the focus of pervasive social discontent; unable to sustain their habitual self-image as tolerable enclaves of disinterested enquiry, they were exposed instead as both locked into and paradigmatic of wider structures of dehumanizing bureaucracy, complicit with military violence and technological exploitation. A more socially heterogeneous student body, products of 'mass culture' rather than 'high literature' and often in instinctive ideological conflict with the assumptions of the ruling academic caste, threatened to atomize and undermine the liberal humanist consensus which was, in effect, criticism's sole rationale. As Elizabeth Bruss has argued in the context of the North American universities:

> One can pick out easily enough the factors that promoted this condition of unrest and suspicion: cooperation between the academy and the military in covert political operations and an overtly unpopular war; a burgeoning of the school population (both students and teachers), especially at the upper levels; and beyond the problem of sheer mass, the problem of a new heterogeneity of ethnic heritage and race and class erupting into what had been the small and traditionally restricted world of higher education . . . Coherence was also threatened by a student body that lacked the common preparatory training, the shared experience of the world, or even the uniform language upon which teachers had formerly been able to draw. Such a setting made notions like 'ordinary language' and 'common sense' increasingly problematic, and the tacit interests and assumptions that had always governed classroom procedures and curricula were suddenly exposed to view. At the same time a subsidized and expanding faculty was producing scholarship at an unprecedented rate and achieving an equally unprecedented degree of specialization, making a 'community of scholars' – with access to the same information – all but impossible. And the fact of subsidy, under-writing all this expansion, made the academy's traditional claim that it was acting as the gadfly of the state ring rather hollow.[104]

What is striking about Bruss's eloquent exposition is that it reproduces, almost point by point, the factors responsible for the erosion of the classical bourgeois public sphere. The increasing 'statification' of the public sphere, as it becomes penetrated by state capital and locked directly into power-structures from which it was traditionally distanced; the consequent shrinkage of an 'autonomous' cultural space which had customarily mediated between the public sphere and material interests, leaving the relations between such interests and the public sphere offensively visible; the increasingly heterogeneous character of the 'public', and the emergence within it of ideological interests incompatible with a received consensus; the fragmentation of knowledge within the traditional intelligentsia under the pressures of specialization: it is as though the narrative of the public sphere's gradual degeneration is dramatically re-run, in greatly compressed form, in the context of higher education. The academy, into which, one might argue, the bourgeois public sphere had migrated in attenuated shape, is now under siege from precisely those forces which had undone the dreams of the Enlightenment. The Leavisian faith that a refurbished public sphere could be launched from the universities themselves was unmasked by the 1960s as a peculiarly grotesque irony.

The ensuing crisis of criticism, as Bruss goes on to point out, was part of a more general failure of credibility in the dominant ideology as a whole:

> Here the fear of 'rationalization as technocratic violence' and the 'quarrel with an industrial society's uses of objectivity' became the basis for outright social struggle. The long romance with humanism, the delight in the masterful imposition of human form on the chaos of nature, had

turned sour . . . the means of mastery seemed to have out-
stripped human desire, and a menacing gap opened up
between a realm of fact without subjective commitment
and a new subjectivity without authority to rule it . . .
Television was perhaps the sole remaining universal, the
only thing that every member of this complex and divided
society could share, yet through it, social relations were
turned into spectacle and reality was defined as an object of
consumption. Thus it is understandable that against this
pervasive sense of personal isolation and passivity, of
social structures aloof, mysterious, and unwieldly, of an
intellectual and technological pursuit of mastery that had
become dangerously self-contained and capable of manu-
facturing its own ends, the various political and student
movements that took shape during the sixties should be for
greater participation in all phases of collective life. And that
fixed hierarchies, received traditions, covert understand-
ings of all types should be anathema.[105]

It was out of the upheavals Bruss describes that the
concerns of contemporary literary theory were born.
Literary theory, in the forms in which we now know it, is
a child of the social and political convulsions of the
1960s. Theory is often enough perceived as an arcane,
sophisticated pursuit, and there is good reason for this;
but to track the development of modern literary theory
back to the 1960s is to remind ourselves of the essential
naivety of all theoretical ventures. The theoretical question always envinces something of the child's puzzle-
ment over practices into which it has not yet been fully
inserted; as long as those practices have not yet become
'naturalized', the child retains a sense of their
mysterious, perhaps even comic arbitrariness and continues to address the most fundamental, intractable
questions about their grounds and motivations to its
wryly amused elders. Those adults will attempt to soothe

the child's bemusement with a Wittgensteinian justification: 'This is just what we *do*, dear'; but the child who
retains its wonderment will grow into the theoretician
and political radical who demands justification, not just
for this or that practice, but for the whole form of
material life – the institutional infrastructure – which
grounds them, and who does not see why it may not be
possible to do things differently for a change. The form
of a philosophical question, Wittgenstein remarks, is 'I
don't know my way around', with the heavy implication
that being handed a map will rectify all such momentary
blunderings. But it is not clear that the adults know their
way around either, even if they *act* as though they do; it
is far from obvious that the arbitrariness and opacity
which the child discerns in their actions is merely a
quality of its own rawness, rather than also, so to speak,
a quality of those actions themselves. The child may
grow up to be, like its elders, a successful actor, fully
internalizing the language games among which it finds
itself; or it may grow up to be a Brechtian actor, whose
behaviour estranges such language games to the point
where their arbitrariness, and hence their transform-
ability, becomes suddenly visible. The genuinely theoretical question is always in this sense violently estran-
ging, a perhaps impossible attempt to raise to self-
reflexivity the very enabling conditions of a range of
routinized practices; and though I have termed such a
question naive, it would be more honest and accurate to
describe it as *faux* naive. The child's impossible questions are no doubt never innocent, embodying as they
do some epistemophilic drive; and the theoretician's
question, similarly, is less wide-eyed than craftily
rhetorical, less the breathless amazement of a Miranda
than the world-weary incredulity at the tenacity of
human folly of the Fool. The theoretical question is

always in this sense a kind of folly in itself; but whereas the Fool has long since resigned himself to the inevitability of mystification, the radical theoretician forms his or her question with a rhetorical inflection which implies the necessity for change. The question is less a polite 'What is going on?' than an impatient 'What the hell is all this?'

'An increase of theoretical activity,' Elizabeth Bruss writes, ' . . . arises whenever the function of criticism is itself in doubt.' Theory, that is, does not emerge at just any historical moment; it comes into being when it is both possible and necessary, when the traditional rationales for a social or intellectual practice have broken down and new forms of legitimization for it are needed. 'At a certain point in the life of these activities,' comments Robert J. Matthews, 'the simple fact that they *are* conducted no longer suffices; the existent sanction must be replaced by a rational one.'[106] The force of that 'must' is not, as I shall argue, incontrovertible; but Matthews, like Bruss, has grasped the most productive way of distinguishing 'theory' from 'ideology'. In the 1960s, which, as Fredric Jameson has argued, ended in 1974,[107] liberal humanism within the academy was challenged as elitist, idealist, depoliticizing and socially marginal. As a professional discipline, it was seen as complicit with the formal systems of social reproduction; as an 'amateur' discourse, it was perceived as historically superannuated. The precarious synthesis of the 'technical' and 'humanistic' which criticism had wrestled from its bedevilled past was in this sense once more split apart. Criticism was guilty both because it was an active force in reproducing the dominant social relations, and because it was impotently tangential to the very social formation it helped to sustain. The new 'politics of knowledge' which the 1960s brought to birth could expose in dialectical fashion both criticism's imbrication in a network of (in Michel Foucault's term) power-knowledge, and the social marginality which nevertheless persisted through this collusion. The contradictoriness of this lay not in the critique, but was inscribed in the nature of criticism itself. For the task of academic criticism, then as now, was to train students in the effective deployment of certain techniques, in the efficient mastery of a certain discourse, as a means of certificating them as intellectually qualified recruits to the ruling class. For this purpose, the 'literary' or 'aesthetic' content of their education was almost wholly beside the point; few of them were likely to find an acquaintance with Baudelaire indispensable for personnel management. The expanding student population of the 1960s, with its consequent rationalizing and reifying of pedagogical methods, its packaged, depersonalized learning, threw into brutal exposure the abstract 'exchange-value' of such training; but at the same stroke it embarrassingly fore-grounded the flagrant discrepancy between the 'exchange-value' of the form of literary education and the much-vaunted 'use-values' of its content. Literary education was a commodity precisely in so far as the former dominated the latter; a correctly sensitive response to the complexities of sexual love or the absurdity of the human condition was the mechanism by which a student might gain his or her niche in Whitehall. Once ensconced there, however, the use-value of such literary humanism was by no means self-evident – which is not to say that it lacked all social function. Literary humanist discourse was certainly a peripheral phenomenon within late capitalism, but this, precisely, was its ordained place. Its role was to *be* marginal: to figure as that 'excess', that supplement to social reality which in Derridean style both revealed and concealed a lack, at once appending itself to an apparently replete social order and unmasking an absence at its heart where the stirrings of repressed desire could be faintly detected. This, surely, is the true locus of 'high culture' in late monopoly capitalism: neither decorative irrelevance nor indispensable ideology, neither structural nor superfluous, but a properly marginal presence, marking the border where that society both encounters and exiles its own disabling absences.

The epistemology of New Critical literary humanism had essayed a certain challenge to the scientific rationalism of bourgeois society. It was the task of criticism, through its complex perceptions of poetic ambiguity, to restore to the world that sensuous particularity of which such rationalism had robbed it, resisting its remorseless abstraction and commodification of experience. But if the relation of subject to object was thereby reinvested with the symbolic, affective dimensions suppressed by a reified social order, that reification was also paradoxically reproduced: the reading subject assumed a contemplative stance before a literary text defined in stringently objectivist terms. Critical analysis mimed the reifying habits of industrial capitalism even as it resisted them; 'disinterested' aesthetic contemplation parodied the very scientism it was out to challenge. Subjected to the rigorously unalterable text, the reading subject of literary humanism was to achieve free, enriched, self-reflective, autonomous identity precisely within a regulative structure which cast him or her as passive and powerless. The forms of subjectivity generated by literary humanism re-enacted the classic paradigms of bourgeois ideology, unequal to the demands of a decade which was reconstituting the subject as active, mobile, multiple, collectivist and participatory. Much of the literary theory which stemmed from the 1960s was accordingly united in its radical anti-objectivism – an impulse which as often as not confounded reified forms of objectivity with objectivity *tout court*. Phenomenology converted the literary work into a subject in its own right, offering the epistemology of reading itself, that erotic coupling or merging of subject and object everywhere absent in social reality, as a lonely compensation for the miseries of commodification. Reader-response theory, with its stress on the reader's active construction of the text, redramatized in the critical realm the democratic-participatory forces now unleashed in political society; its more radical forms dissolved textual objectivity altogether, in a fantastic wish-fulfilment of total mastery over an erstwhile recalcitrant world. Forms of psycho-analytical criticism grasped the text as a mere relay or occasion by which the reading subject curved back to scrutinize his or her own rather more fascinating psychic scenarios. The undermining of objectivism was, often inseparably, a subversion of that related reification, the autonomy of Literature: it is in the egalitarian, pluralistic, anti-hierarchical 1960s that the current concern to deconstruct the distinctions between elite and popular culture, fictive and non-fictive discourse, tragedy and television, first germinated. The structuralist discernment of codes which traversed these compartmentalized objects quite indifferently provided one theoretical rationale for this democratizing project.

Buffeted between a late bourgeois system which exposed it as increasingly anachronistic, and the forces of political opposition, literary humanism could find less and less toe-hold between monopoly capitalism on the one hand and the student movement on the other. Yet literary theory was not without its own political ambiguities, which were to grow more apparent as the 1970s drew on. Part of the appeal of such theory was that it promised to resolve in its own way the structural contradiction which we have seen inscribed within bourgeois criticism from the outset. For theory was at once technically taxing and elaborate, properly scornful of all 'amateur' escapes into 'ordinary language', and at the same time tenaciously engaged with the most general fundamental structures of human culture. Its specialist idioms articulated themes of global depth and range: the subject, the unconscious, language, ideology, history, cognition, signifying systems as a whole. It is a mark of intellectual amateurism that, à la Addison, it regards discrete regions of knowledge and practice as subsumable to a single metalanguage; theory on the whole refused such an illusion, constituting itself instead as an intricate overlapping of technical discourses which could not be reduced to a central essence. What unified those discourses was as much their critical, structural, demystificatory style of thought as any single body of doctrine; there is no logical reason why a semiotician should interest him or herself in developments within Marxism, yet such interchanges are characteristic of the field.

If this was a major gain of literary theory, however, it proved throughout the 1970s to carry with it a signal disadvantage. It proved, in a word, unusually fetishistic. To say this is not to re-echo the customary humanist banality that theory ousts and stands in for literature – that from its modest beginnings it has grown monstrously hubristic, smothering the object it was supposed to mediate. The claim that theory is admissible only in so far as it directly illuminates the literary text is a blatantly policing gesture. The disparate preoccupations now somewhat randomly grouped under the aegis of 'theory' are rich enough in their own right to warrant 'independent' intellectual status; they are not tolerable merely as a mirror of the all-privileged literary work, which their implications in any case far outstrip. The philosophy of history has legitimate concerns of its own, which are not to be certificated only in so far as they throw an immediate light on the battle of Trafalgar. History may indeed from time to time be the direct object of such study; but it may also act as the 'raw material' for such theoretical enquiry, which then becomes a reflection upon, rather than of, history itself. Unless such theoretical enquiry leads to practical consequences of some kind, then it is of course from a materialist viewpoint fruitless; but this relation of theory and practice is considerably more mediated than those who, in the case of literary theory, seek to relegate theory to the humble handmaiden of the text would imagine. It is not always so easy, or so necessary, to decide whether the theory is illuminating the text or the text is developing the theory. This policing of literary theory is in any case an illusion, as such theory is never merely 'literary' in the first place, never inherently restrictable to the elusive ontological object known as literature. To claim that 'literary theory' does not necessarily derive its *raison d'être* from the literary text is not to fall into theoreticism; it is to recognize that what practical effects it might have will be diffused over a much broader field of signifying practice.

Theory was not, then, a fetish in this sense; it was fetishistic because it helped to provide a progressively discredited criticism with a new rationale, and so to displace attention from the more fundamental question of criticism's social functions. There were, broadly speaking, two ways of opposing and outflanking the liberal humanist consensus in the 1960s and '70s. The first was to shift to a radical rather than liberal humanism, demanding a socially relevant criticism, denouncing the cloistered elitism of the academy and developing a more democratic, participatory, subject-centred learning. The second was to oust the subject entirely, to reject even radical humanism as no more than a left inflection of its liberal counterpart, and to oppose to the nebulous amateurism of the academy an unflinchingly analytic armoury of methods. The structural contradiction between 'amateur' and 'professional', humanist and technical, that is to say, reproduced itself within the currents of oppositional criticism – in the case of Marxism, for example, in an increasingly sterile quarrel between Lukács and Althusser. To the 'scientific' camp, the radical humanists marked the extreme edge of the prevailing problematic, mirror-images of what they opposed; to the radical humanists, the 'scientific' critics hoped to dismantle bourgeois ideology with the very reified, technocratic modes of discourse most dear to its heart.

Both of these viewpoints grasped part of the truth, but both were undialectical. The symptomatically rapid flaring and fizzling of radical humanist talk of 'participation', around the years of the Vietnam war, indeed indicated the unstable, largely conjunctural set of forces such talk represented. At the same time, however, radical humanism played a significant role in bringing the Vietnam war to an end. Structuralism and its siblings were indeed in their 'high' period scientistic, enmortgaged to aspects of the very social order which defined them as subversive; yet structuralism's extreme philosophical conventionalism and anti-empiricism were considerably more demystifying affairs. A properly dialectical account has yet to be given of how structuralism was *at once*, in its scientism, functionalism, idealism, compulsive holism, liquidation of history and subjectivity, and reduction of social practice to reified process, an ideology eminently suitable to advanced capitalism, *and simultaneously*, in its full-blooded conventionalism, ruthless demystification of the 'natural', refusal of bourgeois-humanist pieties and exposure of truth as 'production', a limited critique of that very social order. In the event, as the 1970s unrolled, it was structuralism and its progeny which were to prove hegemonic. This was hardly suprising, not only because radical humanism had been rolled back and dissipated with the passing of the liberationist late '60s into the crisis-ridden mid-'70s, but because structuralism, as a theoretical rather than political discourse, was considerably more appropriable by the academy than talk of student power. The crippling consequence of this outcome was that the *institutional* question, so aggressively, theatrically raised by the radical humanism of the earlier period, was effectively lost to theory. An academicized Marxist criticism remained largely silent on this score. It was left to feminist criticism, in some ways the inheritor of late-sixties radical humanism and (in the Anglophone world at least) strenuously anti-structuralist, to maintain this issue on the theoretical agenda.

The advent of deconstruction held the promise of a certain provisional resolution of criticism's problems, much as deconstruction itself would resist any such suggestion of 'closure'. For deconstruction, in a strategically admirable manoeuvre, was at once anti-scientistic and anti-subject. It thus provided something of an ideal position for those who, disenchanted with the metaphysical presuppositions of high structuralism, nonetheless cherished its anti-humanism. It was now possible to outflank liberal humanism, radical humanism and scientism at a stroke, as each had previously sought to outflank the other. There were, however, a number of difficulties with this audacious surpassing. Deconstruc-

tion had its root in France – in a society whose ruling ideologies drew freely upon a metaphysical rationalism incarnate in the rigidly hierarchical, authoritarian nature of its academic institutions. In this context, the Derridean project of dismantling binary oppositions and subverting the transcendental signifier had a radical potential relevance which did not always survive when deconstruction was exported. The creed, in short, did not travel well: transplanted to the liberal empiricist rather than rationalistic cultures of Britain and North America, its complicity with liberal humanism tended to bulk as large as its antagonism to it. If I may be allowed to quote an earlier comment of my own on this point: 'The modest disownment of theory, method and system; the revulsion from the dominative, totalizing, and un-equivocally denotative; the privileging of plurality and heterogeneity, the recurrent gestures of hesitation and indeterminacy, the devotion to gliding and process, slip-page and movement; the distaste for the definitive – it is not difficult to see why such an idiom should become so quickly absorbed within the Anglo-Saxon academies.'[108] That final phrase is in fact grossly overstated, confound-ing a tendency with a *fait accompli*: such absorption is by no means as yet the rule in either Britain or America, and the comment merely ignores those aspects of decon-struction which are indeed unsettling to the dominant ideologies. The epistemological scepticism and his-torical relativism of certain militant forms of deconstruc-tion are profoundly antithetical to academic orthodoxy, shaking as they do the very foundations of scholarly objectivity. It would perhaps be more accurate to argue that the Anglophone varieties of deconstruction rejoin the liberalism of the ruling critical ideology at the very moment that they challenge its humanism – that such deconstruction is, in short, a liberalism without a subject, and as such, among other things, an appropriate ideological form for late capitalist society. Classical liberalism was always wracked by a conflict between the autonomy of the self and its plurality, seeking to fold back the latter within the regulative unity of the former; deconstruction takes up this contradiction, in a later stage of bourgeois society where the humanist doctrine of autonomy is increasingly implausible and discredited, and boldly sacrifices that traditional liberal shibboleth to the cause of a plurality which might just give ideology the slip. Ideological closure can no longer be opposed by the free, positive self-fulfilments of the individual; but it might be countered instead by the more negative free play of the signifier, which can escape the deathly embrace of some terroristic meaning exactly as the liberal self once hopelessly believed it might do. In a curious historical irony, the death of the free subject is now an essential condition for the preservation of that freedom in transformed style. Deconstruction rescues the heterogeneity of the subject from its hypostatization, but only at the cost of liquidating the subjective agency which might engage, politically rather than textually, with the very ideological systems which necessitated this strategy in the first place. It is for this reason that it reproduces a blending of bleakness and euphoria, affirmation and resignation, characteristic of the liberal humanist tradition. Nothing is more striking in Leavis's 'great tradition' than the ideological filter which selects for such status literary texts which combine the liberal subject's rich, giddying sense of its own transgressive powers with a paralytic awareness of its inexorable subjection to oppressive systems. Deconstruction's dual sensibility, at once stoically conformed to the ineluctability of metaphysics and enraptured by a *jouissance* or *mise-en-abyme* which promises to shatter

that whole enclosure, has doubtless a particular historical source: it mixes the left pessimism of the post-
1968 period with a discourse which continues, as it were,
to keep the revolution warm. But it also echoes the form
sensibility of traditional liberalism itself, divided as it is,
to adopt a formulation of Paul de Man's, into 'an empirical self that exists in a state of inauthenticity and a
self that exists only in the form of a language that asserts
the knowledge of this inauthenticity.' What for de
Man is the irony of the human condition as such is in fact
the product of a particular historical blockage, of which
deconstruction is the inheritor. The only authentic bourgeois subject is the one who recognizes that transcendence is a myth. The model liter accepts his sentence,
abandoning all foolish dreams of climbing the wall. In
recognizing that bourgeois dreams of transcendence
tend to be foolish fictions, de Man is perfectly correct.
What he does not acknowledge is the equally ideological
character of an irony which gazes contemplatively at the
whole inauthentic scene, wryly conscious of its own
inescapable complicity with what it views, reduced to a
truth which consists in no more than a naming of the
void between its own speech-act and the empirical self.
No more familiar image of the bourgeois liberal could in
fact be conceived; the line from the crippled, marginalized, self-ironizing humanists of Eliot, James and
Forster to the anti-humanist deconstructor is direct and
unbroken. It is because de Man consistently reduces
historicity to empty temporality that he displaces the
dilemmas of the liberal intellectual under late capitalism
into an irony structural to discourse as such
    Only such irony, it would seem, can hope to give
ideology the slip. But what form of ideology is in question here? Behind the deconstructive practice of the so-
called Yale school would seem not to loom the shape of

that whole enclosure, has doubtless a particular historical source: it mixes the left pessimism of the post-1968 period with a discourse which continues, as it were, to keep the revolution warm. But it also echoes the torn sensibility of traditional liberalism itself, divided as it is, to adopt a formulation of Paul de Man's, into 'an empirical self that exists in a state of inauthenticity and a self that exists only in the form of a language that asserts the knowledge of this inauthenticity'.[109] What for de Man is the irony of the human condition as such is in fact the product of a particular historical blockage, of which deconstruction is the inheritor. The only authentic bourgeois subject is the one who recognizes that transcendence is a myth. The model lifer accepts his sentence, abandoning all foolish dreams of climbing the wall. In recognizing that bourgeois dreams of transcendence tend to be foolish fictions, de Man is perfectly correct. What he does not acknowledge is the equally ideological character of an irony which gazes contemplatively at the whole inauthentic scene, wryly conscious of its own inescapable complicity with what it views, reduced to a truth which consists in no more than a naming of the void between its own speech-act and the empirical self. No more familiar image of the bourgeois liberal could in fact be conceived; the line from the crippled, marginalized, self-ironizing humanists of Eliot, James and Forster to the anti-humanist deconstructor is direct and unbroken. It is because de Man consistently reduces historicity to empty temporality that he displaces the dilemmas of the liberal intellectual under late capitalism into an irony structural to discourse as such.

Only such irony, it would seem, can hope to give ideology the slip. But what form of ideology is in question here? Behind the deconstructive practice of the so-called Yale school would seem to loom not the shape of

North American pragmatism and liberal empiricism, but a far more minatory shadow, that of the holocaust. Harold Bloom is a Jew; Geoffrey Hartman is of central European Jewish provenance; de Man's uncle, an ultimately disillusioned socialist, was politically involved in the Second World War period. Only J. Hillis Miller is exceptional here. Ideology for the Yale school would seem in the first place to signify fascism and Stalinism; it is to that traumatic experience, one imagines, that much of their anxiety over the transcendental signifier, totalized system, historical teleology, self-evident truth and 'naturalization' of the contingencies of consciousness can be traced back. It is in this, rather than in their unAmerican familiarity with Husserl and Binswanger, Blanchot and Benjamin, that the Yale school are most significantly European. Whereas the later Frankfurt school, whom the Yale group is certain ways resemble, found only ambiguous refuge from fascism in a supposedly monolithic, inexorably 'administered' American capitalism, the Yale deconstructionists have been able to effect a more fruitful·commerce between North American bourgeois liberalism and a certain selective reading of Derrida – one which, most glaringly, eradicates all traces of the political from his work. Even so, it is not, formally at least, the political which they wish to combat: Hartman has explicitly repudiated such an accusation, and there is evidence that de Man believed himself to be a socialist. It is the ideological, not the political, which is the enemy. But to select Stalinism and fascism as prototypes of the ideological is drastically reductive and essentialistic. For it is simply false to believe that all ideologies, in some structurally invariant manner, rely as profoundly upon apodictic truth, metaphysical groundedness, teleological vision and the violent erasure of difference as these brutally extreme models would sug-

as the view that lectures are a form of violence. For what after all could be more unanswerably authoritative than a discourse which, in the very act of pulling the carpet from under its opponents, presents them with a profile so attenuated that there is no place to hit it, which cannot be knocked down because it is always already sprawling helplessly on the floor? No more aggressive form of *kenosis* could be imagined, short of James's later heroines. In this sense too, deconstruction rejoins traditional liberal humanism, whose serene indulgence of its own befuddlement was always an unmistakable sign of the privilege of those who can afford not to know. There is little admirable in an authority which can immolate itself only because it is always already in place – which can savour the delights of textual agnosticism precisely because it is institutionally secure, and perhaps likely to reinforce that security the more flamboyantly it parades its blindness. Others may not know, but to know that nobody knows is the most privileged knowledge conceivable, well worth trading for a handful of critical certainties. In a period in which, with the decline of the public sphere, the traditional authority of criticism has been called into serious question, a reaffirmation of that authority is urgently needed; but this cannot take the form of reinventing the classical clerisy, with its intuitive and thus dogmatic assurances, for no such model was capable of surviving the demise of *Scrutiny*. The only tolerable gesture of authority, accordingly, becomes self-molesting and self-abnegating – one which combines the authoritarian abrasiveness of informing you that you do not know what you are saying, with the humility of acknowledging that this very statement is by the same token utterly suspect. In this way deconstruction is able to outflank every existing knowledge to absolutely no effect. Like some other modern philo-

gest. Nor is it in the least the case that all ideology is 'naturalizing' – a dogmatic emphasis which the Yale school have inherited from Lukács – or that structures of ironic self-distantiation may not be embedded at its heart. The implicit model of ideology advanced by much deconstruction is, in fact, a straw target, and one which gravely underestimates the complexity and 'textuality' of ideology's operations. No simple binary opposition can be established between 'ideology' – conceived as relentlessly closed and seamlessly self-identical – and *écriture*. Deconstruction's failure to dismantle such an opposition is the surest sign of its own ideological character, and of its collusiveness with the liberal humanism it seeks to embarrass. If the exiled Frankfurt school were haunted by an experience of ideology which they then erroneously extended to liberal bourgeois society, the Yale school, mesmerized by much the same model, would seem insufficiently aware of those ideological practices which do not fall under this rubric.

If criticism is in crisis, then as Paul Bové has suggested, 'Is deconstruction not the perfect institutional response to this crisis (rather than its cause)? Is it not a strategy for taking up the crisis into the academy in a self-preserving act which, as Donald Pease has suggested, fuels the institution with its own impotence?'[110] One is reminded of the anthropological tale of the tiger which regularly disrupted a tribal ceremony by leaping into its midst; after a while, the tiger was incorporated into the ritual. It is certainly tempting to see Anglophone deconstruction as that crisis theorized, canonized, internalized, gathered up into the academy as a new set of textual techniques or fresh injection of intellectual capital to eke out its dwindling resources. The deconstructionist disownment of authority is plainly in line with the politics of the '60s; yet it is nothing so simplistic

sophy, it cancels all the way through and leaves everything just as it was. To safeguard its radicalism, it cannot
settle for being no more than a set of traditional liberal
caveats, issuing prudent warnings against all undue
absolutizing, for then how does it differ in effect from
the language of a Lionel Trilling or a John Bayley? Yet if it
attempts to be more than this, to distance itself implacably from its embarrassing affinities with the nominalist, anti-totalizing, untheoretical, differential ideology
of a Bayley, it is at risk of undercutting its own anti-
absolutist currents and launching 'wilder' claims - truth,
identity, community, meaning are mere illusions, which
are no more than a negative metaphysic. The upshot of
deconstruction is thus, as I have argued elsewhere, the
impasse of an opposition ceaselessly, irresolvably
divided between its reformist and ultra-leftist
moments.

What survives Yale deconstruction's apparent
abnegation of authority, at least in the work of a de Man,
is a view of the relations between literature and other
discourses which is an exact mirror-image of liberal
humanist orthodoxy. There is no question of dislodging
that orthodoxy's faith in the centrality of literature: on
the contrary, literature becomes the truth, essence or
self-consciousness of all other discourses precisely
because, unlike them, it knows that it does not know
what it is talking about. Indeed the more hopelessly at
sea it becomes, the more supremely central it grows; the
liberal humanist's view of literary 'content' is cancelled
while his sense of the formal relations between literature
and other idioms is reproduced. Literature, paradoxically, becomes the centre from which all centring is
denounced, the truth by which all truth may be deconstructed. At one time the very image of totality, it is now
the dissolution of it: if it has altered its function, it has

sophy, it cancels all the way through and leaves everything just as it was. To safeguard its radicalism, it cannot settle for being no more than a set of traditional liberal *caveats*, issuing prudent warnings against all undue absolutizing, for then how does it differ in effect from the language of a Lionel Trilling or a John Bayley? Yet if it attempts to be more than this, to distance itself implacably from its embarrassing affinities with the nominalist, anti-totalizing, untheoretical, differential ideology of a Bayley, it is at risk of undercutting its own anti-absolutist *caveats* and launching 'wilder' claims – truth, identity, continuity, meaning are mere illusions – which are no more than a negative metaphysic. The *aporia* of deconstruction is thus, as I have argued elsewhere, the impasse of an opposition ceaselessly, irresolvably divided between its 'reformist' and 'ultra-leftist' moments.

What survives Yale deconstruction's apparent abnegation of authority, at least in the work of a de Man, is a view of the relations between literature and other discourses which is an exact mirror-image of liberal humanist orthodoxy. There is no question of dislodging that orthodoxy's faith in the centrality of literature; on the contrary, literature becomes the truth, essence or self-consciousness of all other discourses precisely because, unlike them, it knows that it does not know what it is talking about. Indeed the more hopelessly at sea it becomes, the more supremely central it grows; the liberal humanist's view of literary 'content' is cancelled, while his sense of the formal relations between literature and other idioms is reproduced. Literature, paradoxically, becomes the centre from which all centring is denounced, the truth by which all truth may be deconstructed. At one time the very image of totality, it is now the dissolution of it; if it has altered its function, it has not shifted its locus. Whereas literature for *Scrutiny* was the central touchstone which revealed all other languages as anaemically absent, unable to flesh their abstractions into concrete presence, literature for de Man exposes its discursive bedfellows as repellently present, languishing in the grip of a logocentrism which is the very measure of their inauthenticity. Whether literature claims a negative or positive knowledge, then, it remains all-privileged, and the continuity between bourgeois humanism and deconstruction stays to that extent unbroken.

Purely 'textual' deconstruction of the Yale variety draws at least two benefits from the notion that criticism, like language itself, is somehow always in crisis. On the one hand, this move helps to occlude the specificity of the historical crisis criticism now confronts, dissolving it to a generalized irony of discourse and so relieving deconstruction of the responsibilities of historical self-reflection. On the other hand, the fact that we are always in crisis secures deconstruction a safe, indeed interminable future: The deconstructive gesture, Hillis Miller has argued, always fails, 'so that it has to be performed again and again, interminably . . . '[11] This is certainly a reassuring kind of failure to run up against – one that promises to keep you in a job indefinitely, unlike those research programmes which frustratingly run out of steam just as you are about to gain promotion. Since no deconstructive critical text will be quite purged of some particles of positivity, a further text will always be needed to dissolve these away, and that in turn be vulnerable to another, for as long as blank pages are unacceptable as scholarly publications. If the effect of such deconstruction is the interminable reproduction of the academy, however, there is a deconstructive left wing which has indeed acknowledged, however nominally, the problem of deconstructing that institution itself. The politics of such left deconstruction have been characteristically anarchistic: a suspicion of power, authority and institutional forms *as such,* which is once more a radical inflection of liberalism. Such an institutional critique is bound to be formalist and abstract, as well as covertly moralistic; but it is also possible to see a certain post-structuralist fixation on power as such as the reflection of a real historical problem. For once the ruling liberal humanist ideology of the academic institutions has been called into question – once it is assumed that such liberal humanism is indeed increasingly anachronistic – then it is not easy to see exactly *how* the academy contributes to the reproduction of broader ideological relations, granted that this question is not itself brusquely dismissed as 'functionalist'. It becomes plausible, in other words, to regard such institutions as deploying power for its own sake, self-fuelling machines whose power-struggles have a purely internal reference, in a period when the ideological relations between academy and society are more complex, ambiguous and opaque than many earlier radical models supposed. If deconstruction is telling academic liberal humanism that it does not know quite what it is doing, or whether it is doing anything or not, or whether it can know whether it is doing anything or not, then this is not only because of the tropical, fictive nature of all discourse; it is also because of an historical uncertainty in the wider social functions of academic humanism, which neither it, nor much deconstruction, will fully acknowledge.

VI

I began this essay by arguing that modern criticism was born of a struggle against the absolutist state. It has ended up, in effect, as a handful of individuals reviewing each other's books. Criticism itself has become incorporated into the culture industry, as a 'type of unpaid public relations, part of the requirements in any large corporate undertaking'.[112] In the early eighteenth century, to risk an excessive generalization, criticism concerned cultural politics; in the nineteenth century its preoccupation was public morality; in our own century it is a matter of 'literature'. As Robert Weimann complains, 'academic critics have largely abandoned the broadly civilizing function of criticism.'[113] Yet is is arguable that criticism was only ever significant when it engaged with more than literary issues – when, for whatever historical reason, the 'literary' was suddenly foregrounded as the medium of vital concerns deeply rooted in the general intellectual, cultural and political life of an epoch. The period of the Enlightenment, the drama of Romanticism and the moment of *Scrutiny* are exemplary cases in point. It has only been when criticism, in the act of speaking of literature, emits a lateral message about the shape and destiny of a whole culture that its voice has compelled widespread attention. It was only when 'cul-

ture' became a pressing political project, 'poetry' a metaphor for the quality of social life, and language a paradigm for social practice as a whole, that criticism could
claim any serious title to exist. Today, apart from its
marginal role in reproducing the dominant social relations through the academies, it is almost entirely bereft
of such a *raison d'être*. It engages at no significant point
with any substantive social interest, and as a form of
discourse is almost entirely self-validating and self-
perpetuating. It is hard to believe that, in a nuclear age,
the publication of yet another study of Robert Herrick is
justifiable. Should criticism, then, be allowed to wither
away, or can some more productive role be discovered
for it? TO ILLUMINATE
" PROVIDE PROFOUND UNDERSTANDING

The single most important critic of post-war Britain has
been Raymond Williams. Yet 'critic' in its contemporary
meaning is for him a problematic description, and he
has for several years now explicitly rejected the appella-
tion of *literary* critic. None of the other conventional
labels – sociologist, political theorist, social philosopher,
cultural commentator – fits his work exhaustively or
exactly. The transgression of borders has been a recurrent metaphor in his writing, which has ranged across
theatre and linguistics, literature and politics, education
and popular culture, film, ecology and political nationa-
lism. The frontier between 'critical' and 'creative'
writing has been equally flouted: Williams is novelist,
dramatist and (early in his career) film scriptwriter, and
his non-fictional work displays an intense 'imaginative'
charge and uniquely experiental emphasis which allows
it to veer easily into rhetoric and narrative. Aside from
the somewhat uninformative title of 'cultural studies',
there is as yet no precise name for the area Williams
inhabits, an area of which he was indeed one of the

architects. He is not a 'discourse theorist' or semiotician, since though language has been one of his most persistent pre-occupations he has always refused to divorce the study of it from an enquiry into social and cultural institutions as a whole. In this way as in others, Williams's work has prefigured and pre-empted the development of parallel left positions by, so to speak, apparently standing still. When structuralism and semiotics were most in fashion, Williams abided by his concern with the 'non-discursive' only to see the erstwhile devotees of structuralism rejoining him in their discovery of Voloshinov and Foucault. While other materialist thinkers, including myself, diverted into structuralist Marxism, Williams sustained his historicist humanism only to find such theoreticians returning under changed political conditions to examine that case less cavalierly, if not to endorse it uncritically. Williams's interest in the material institutions of culture pre-dated the popularity of cultural studies, as his then unfashionable care for the natural environment anticipated the ecological movement. The project of a 'semantic materialism' was implicit in his work almost from the outset, as was a rejection of any purely 'literary' focus: two of his earliest texts were devoted respectively to theatre and film.

If Williams is not a professional historian, sociologist, or political theorist, neither can he be branded as an amateur. There are, perhaps inevitably, patches of his work which suffer from insufficient technical knowledge and a lack of rigorous theorization; but there is no sense in which Williams extends himself over these immensely diverse fields by the deployment of a metalanguage into which they can all be smoothly subsumed. In his global moral concern he is to some extent an inheritor of the lineage of nineteenth-century moralists he records in *Culture and Society 1780–1950*; indeed the remarkable Conclusion to that work, with its span, depth and political wisdom, recalls some of the finest pronouncements of that tradition. But Williams's generalizing capacity is for the most part closely linked to a tenaciously detailed cultural and historical knowledge, quite different in method – if not always in its occasionally Olympian tone – from the Victorian sage. Williams's synoptic view is not that of the transcendental observer who has grasped the essence of the totality, but one which derives from examining the *articulations* between different sign-systems and practices. His early concept of a 'structure of feeling' is vital in this respect, mediating as it does between an historical set of social relations, the general cultural and ideological modes appropriate to them, and the specific forms of subjectivity (embodied not least in artefacts) in which such modes are lived out. If Williams has a 'field', then it is doubtless this: the space constituted by the interaction of social relations, cultural institutions and forms of subjectivity. The name of this field can be left to the academics to decide.

Responding to an enquiry about his cultural perspectives in the years immediately after the Second World War, Williams comments:

> I thought that the Labour government had a choice: either for reconstruction of the cultural field in capitalist terms, or for funding institutions of popular education and popular culture that could have withstood the political campaigns in the bourgeois press that were already gathering momentum. In fact, there was a rapid option for conventional capitalist priorities; the refusal to finance the documentary film movement was an example. I still believe that the failure to fund the working-class movement culturally when the channels of popular education and popular

culture were there in the forties became a key factor in the very quick disintegration of Labour's position in the fifties. I don't think you can understand the projects of the New Left in the late fifties unless you realize that people like Edward Thompson and myself, for all our differences, were positing the re-creation of that kind of union. Perhaps by that date it was no longer available. But our perspective seemed to us a reasonable one, even though it would have been very hard to achieve.[114]

How far William's expectations of the post-war Labour government were politically realistic is, of course, a matter for debate. But the absence of institutions of popular culture and education he indicates here was to have a crucial effect upon his own work. Williams's most seminal early text, *Culture and Society 1780–1950*, was produced in effective political isolation – in the context of 'a breakdown of any collective project that (he) could perceive, political, literary or cultural'. The work was marked, in his own words, by 'elements of a disgusted withdrawal . . . from all immediate forms of collaboration, combined – and this eventually made the difference – with an intense disappointment that they were not available . . .'[115] As the 1950s drew on, Williams was to experience such collaboration with the rise of the New Left, and the 1960s and early '70s brought with them a resurgence of political thought and practice which was to provide some context for his own intellectual work. The scars of that early sceptical dissociation, however, were never to be quite eradicated: the experience had perhaps proved too formative and definitive, so that even Williams's later work, produced in a period when the political conditions for action and collaboration were more propitious, was carried on at a certain aloof distance from those arenas.

10 - 18 - 05
FAMILY
FURNITURE
ATTITUDES
REVEALED

Williams's writing, that is to say, dramatizes in its very style, sometimes in peculiarly intense form, the major problem confronting all socialist intellectual work today: that it is in some sense addressed to an absent counterpublic sphere, one based upon those very institutions of popular culture and education which failed to emerge in post-war Britain. Lest such a notion be dismissed as a left-academic fantasy, a glance at a very different historical situation is perhaps necessary. In the Weimar Republic, the working-class movement was not only a redoubtable political force; it was also equipped with its own theatres and choral societies, clubs and newspapers, recreation centres and social forums. It was these conditions which helped to make possible a Brecht and a Benjamin, and to shift the role of critic from isolated intellectual to political functionary. In the Britain of the 1930s, *agitprop* groups, the Unity theatre, the Workers' Film and Photo League, The Workers' Theatre Movement, workplace branches of the Left Book Club, the London Workers' Film Society and a range of other institutions reflected elements of this rich counterculture. It was just such a counterpublic sphere, however undeveloped and uneven, of which Williams, as a postwar socialist intellectual, was damagingly bereft. Like others of us, but more poignantly and dramatically, he was driven instead to occupy an indeterminate space mid-way between an actual but reactionary academy and a desirable but absent counterpublic sphere. In fact, of course, his influence has always extended considerably beyond the academy: to denigrate as an 'academicist' writer a man whose books had by 1979 sold some 750,000 copies in Britain alone requires a curious twist of logic. But in the virtual absence of a counterpublic sphere, that readership could not be politically organized; the reception and discussion of Williams's work could not be part of a broader politico-cultural project, linked to actual cultural experiments and interventions. In the effective absence of a working-class theatre movement, Williams's political drama found a home instead, for both good and ill, in the capitalist media; in the absence of working-class institutions of literary and intellectual production, one of the most vital tasks of the socialist intellectual – that of the resolute popularization of complex ideas, conducted within a shared medium which forbids patronage and condescension – was denied him. For genuine political popularization involves more than producing works which make socialist theory intelligible to a mass audience, important though that project is; such a readership must be institutionalized rather than amorphous, able to receive and interpret such work in a collective context and to ponder its consequences for political action. The simple, glaring lack of a popular socialist newspaper in Britain, which is not of course the result of an oversight on the part of socialist intellectuals, has deprived Williams of one major potential contribution to the construction of a counterpublic sphere.

The Victorian man of letters worked within institutions which put him in unusually close touch with the social class of which he was representative. Although, as we have seen, that audience was felt to be increasingly fragmented and uneven, it retained for a while enough common identity of interests for the man of letters to experience his role as socially defined rather than individually created. Through a network of personal and professional contacts, he had indirect access to the levers of political power and the centres of policy-making. Williams's work has the range of the man of letters; but the location of the socialist critic in late capitalism is inevitably quite different from that of a Morley or

Stephen. He or she is askew to that society rather than representative of it; and to this extent, paradoxically, he resembles less the man of letters than the isolated, dissentient sage. That this has been an element in Williams's popular image is not without significance. There are, in fact, interesting parallels between his career and that of Wordsworth – without, of course, the latter's political apostasy. Both offer an autobiographical experience of personal growth within a rural community as a moral and social critique of the given social order; both are consequently wedded to an ethic of authentic experience, an aesthetic of realism and an ecological sense of creative social relations; both endured an alienating encounter with ruling-class Cambridge, and moved in this period towards revolutionary politics; both returned finally to rural environments. Similarities of sensibility could also be outlined, as well as a shared strain of populism. But if neither socialist nor Romantic writer can assume an existing audience, the socialist cannot fall prey to the Romantic illusion that such an audience can be actively constituted by his or her own work; for the 'audience' of socialism is to a large extent politically predetermined and pre-given, not just those who share a sensibility but those who occupy a common social location. The Romantic poet seeks a pact between his own discourse and a common culture in the face of the political; for the socialist critic, the political is the precondition of such solidarity. Socialist criticism cannot conjure a counterpublic sphere into existence; on the contrary, that criticism cannot itself fully exist until such a sphere has been fashioned. Until that time, the socialist critic will remain stranded between sage and man of letters, combining the critical dissociation of the former with the practical, engaged, wide-ranging activity of the latter. The very term 'intellectual', suggestive as it is of both critical detachment and synoptic engagement, captures something of this paradox. The borders which Raymond Williams's work has finally been unable to cross are not those between intellectual disciplines, politics and literature, or critical and 'creative' writing; they are the frontiers between the academic institution and political society, which the absence of a counterpublic sphere throws into graphic relief.

Distinct from both state and public sphere in the eighteenth-century is a third realm, which Jürgen Habermas terms the 'intimate' sphere of family and household. The 'intimate' sphere is not part of the public sphere, relegated as the post-feudalist family now is to the area of privacy; but it provides, nonetheless, a vital source of impulses and energies for that more public arena. If the English coffee houses, unlike the French salons, excluded women – who were moved at times to produce polemical pamphlets on the social evils of coffee-drinking – it was because 'culture' in early eighteenth-century England was assuming social and political functions from which women were debarred. In a cynical twist of history, women were formally admitted to the political public sphere with their achievement of the vote in 1928 at a point when that sphere was now in effect anachronistic. Though the bourgeois public sphere officially excluded the 'intimate' realm, however, it was in other ways deeply enmortgaged to it. For the eighteenth-century public sphere thematizes and consolidates forms of subjectivity which have their root in the domestic world. That world generates new forms of subjectivity which are, in Habermas's phrase, 'publicly oriented', and which then pass over into the male-dominated public sphere to attain self-reflective formulation. No clearer example of this could be found than in the deliberations of Samuel Richardson's famous female coterie – deliberations which, through continuous, collective, 'rational' discussion, crystallize modes of intimate feeling and behaviour which are then objectifiable as public forms. The focus of such discussions was, of course, literature; and that this is so suggests something of the prime importance of literature, then as now. Literature was a vital nexus or mediation between the now privatized nuclear family and the political public sphere; it provided the symbolic forms for the negotiation of new modes of subjectivity, which could then be transmitted into the public domain. At once experiential and reflective, deeply inward yet formally regulated, literature occupied a privileged space mid-way between the depths of the autonomous subject and the institutional life of political society. The bourgeois novel, as Habermas notes, evolves from the epistolary form – from private letters within and between families, which gradually achieve more publicly relevant status. Yet the process is naturally more dialectical than this: literature is not merely the 'reflection' of the intimate realm in more public guise, but an active constituent of that domestic sphere, teaching modes of feeling and relationship which are drawn back into the family, intervening to reorganize the arena of intimacy into subjective forms appropriate to the social and political goals of early capitalism. The role of 'culture' is to generate new forms of subjectivity by a ceaseless mediation between two dimensions of social life – the family and political society – which have now been defined as distinct.

Such distinctness is in part, of course, an ideological illusion, albeit one of remarkable efficacy. The 'autonomy' of the family is as hollow as the 'autonomy' of the public sphere itself, and in some ways parallels it. Both realms constitute themselves as separate from political society on the basis of their complicity with it. 'The individual-private sphere, as Nicos Poulantzas has written, 'is created by the State concomitantly with its relative separation from the public space of society . . . The individual-private forms an integral part of the strategic field constituted by the modern State, which fixes it as the target of its power. In short, it exists only in and through the State.'[116] If what is at stake in the public sphere is neither power nor rank but the very essence of civilized reason, then beneath this deceptive equality, nurturing it continually, lies an even more profound homogeneity: that of the 'human' itself, whose home is the family hearth. In their hearts, in the company of their wives and daughters, all bourgeois are as one. The ideology of the family serves in the eighteenth century to mask domestic power-relations, and their interlocking with the systems of bourgeois property, just as the ideology of the public sphere serves to mask the exploitation of civil society.

As bourgeois society develops into the modern epoch, the relations between public sphere, 'intimate' sphere and state undergo significant changes. With the increasing 'statification' of the public sphere, the 'intimate' sphere becomes progressively marginalized; state education and social policy take over many of the functions previously reserved to the family, blurring the boundaries between 'public' and 'private' and stripping the family of its social, productive roles. The 'intimate' sphere is in this sense deprivatized, pulled into public society – but only, in a notable historical irony, to be reprivatized as a unit of consumption. Private consumption and leisure, based upon the now shrunken space of the family, replace the forms of social discussion previously associated with the public sphere. The emergence of the women's movement can be seen as, among other things, a response to these changed conditions. For if the family is no longer the privileged site of subjectivity it once was, if experience within the 'intimate' sphere has itself become commodified, and if that sphere has been increasingly incorporated into the state, then the feminist demand for the full socialization of the family moves with the historical grain at the very moment that it conflicts with the domestic ideologies which mask that material evolution. Such an argument needs severe qualification: it is not at all clear, for example, that the family does not still remain in some ways an important site of subjectivity; and it is not only domestic ideology, but the material gains which accrue to capitalism from the preservation of the family, which block feminist demands on this issue. Even so, the women's movement has reformulated in a historic move the relations between public and 'intimate' spheres. In a striking historical irony, a marginalization of the 'intimate' realm closely related to the decline of the public sphere has led to a fresh resurgence of that realm in the form of a new counterpublic sphere: that of feminist discourse and practice. As with the classical public sphere, distinctions of class may be temporarily suspended, though not ignored, within this new domain: the shared fact of gender works to equalize all participants within it. As with the classical public sphere, 'culture' is once more a vital nexus between politics and personal experience, mediating human needs and desires into publicly discussable form, teaching new modes of subjectivity and combating received representations.

It would be dangerous to press such an analogy too far. One of the most notable limits of Habermas's concept of the public sphere, when offered by his later work as some prefigurement of a socialist future, is its rationalistic character. Such a model would seem to extend, rather than radically to transform, the structures of bourgeois rationality itself, conceived of as some quasi-transcendental capacity. This is markedly untrue of the women's movement. The increasing socialization of the body has led feminism to a 'politics of the body' which is strictly incompatible with any such rationalism. The discourse of the bourgeois public sphere, as of male rationality more generally, is essentially a mingling of disembodied minds, freed from their libidinal encasements just as they are untainted by the pressures of material interest. Such discourse may have been viewed by the eighteenth century as rhetorical in one sense of the term: directed towards persuasion; but it could not be seen as rhetorical in the deeper meaning of the word: inscribed, like all discourse, with the movements of power and desire. The language of feminism, by contrast, is self-consciously rhetorical in this sense, unmasking the reified objectivity of the public sphere's familiar idiom, and so lending itself more obviously to 'cultural' forms. There is a considerable distance between this language and the later Habermas's search for a universal theory of felicitous speech acts.

The rise of the women's movement, then, is one example of the emergence of a counterpublic sphere. Within its space, previously repressed or inarticulate needs, interests and desires find political and symbolic form, mediated by changed idioms, practices and cultural modes. It is just such an articulation of censored personal experience that Oskar Negt and Alexander Kluge see as providing the basis of a proletarian public sphere, which would not be co-extensive with the institutions of organized labour.[117] Within such an arena, authentic needs and desires which at present find distorted expression in the family would be given new form and direction. The importance of this becomes clear if we consider once more the destiny of 'culture' under capitalism, all the way from an early stage of commodity production which allowed art to achieve a certain autonomy, to a late monopoly capitalism which colonizes the very realm of subjectivity itself. John Brenkman has argued that the capitalist mode of production has from this viewpoint evolved by transforming, in two phases, the relation between the economic and the symbolic dimensions of social life. In the first stage, economic and symbolic dimensions are sharply dissevered: industrial capitalist production strips labour of all affective, symbolic connotations, uprooting it from the context of traditional sanctions, rights and obligations it knew under feudalism. 'It separates from this activity all other expenditures of the body's energy, which, having been designated unproductive, manifest themselves in forms of erotic, aesthetic and religious experience.'[118] This division passes into the human subject, bifurcating the producer's relation to the body: 'Set against this instrumentalized body (of the wage-labourer) is the subject's relation to the erotogenic body with its complex network of ties to the symbolic formations and affective experiences that comprise the whole of social experience. Late capitalism overcomes the sheer separation of the symbolic from the economic, but does so by bringing the symbolic under the dominance of the economic. The processes of this subsumption are precisely designed to block the overcoming of the subjective divisions inaugurated by capital.'[119] It is here that the cultural processes of late capitalism are most crucial: 'Through its dominant *cultural* forms and practices, late capitalism strives to sever social experience from the formation of counter-ideologies, to break collective experience into the monadic isolation of the private experiences of individuals, and to pre-empt the effects of association by subsuming the discourses and images that regulate social life.'[120] Whereas capitalism originally pulled material production away from the spheres in which meanings are produced – the condition of the classical public sphere – it has now returned to reorganize the very production of meanings according to the logic of the commodity. If in developed capitalism the political authority of the state intervenes in the social arena of commodity exchange, so certain social forces – 'mass culture' – come to assume political functions.

The role of mass culture, then, is to 'seize upon discourses that are connected to social experience and rework them into a discourse that disperses the subjects it addresses just as it homogenizes the diverse collective articulations that those subjects produce.'[121] Mass culture, if I may elaborate on Brenkman's argument, to some degree displaces the family as the arena in which needs and desires are negotiated, and indeed progressively penetrates the family itself. In the classical public sphere, private experience provided the very basis of public association: participants encountered each other precisely as private citizens, and the subjective autonomy of each was the very structure of their social discourse. The 'intimate' realm of the family and household was at once a refuge from this world, and one matrix of its modes of subjecthood. In late capitalism, privatization becomes the dissolution, not the enabling condition, of public association; it is at once the effect of a real separation between family and society – of the absence of a public sphere which might mediate between them – and, paradoxically, of that deprivatization of the family brought about by the absorption of some of its traditional functions into the state, which maroons the family with little beyond its affective and consumptional experience. The family remains in part a refuge from civil society, nurturing vital impulses unfulfilled by it; but since it is also ceaselessly penetrated by commodity culture, this potentially positive arena of the personal is continually caught up with forms of privatization which atomize, serialize and disconnect. At the same time, the forms of public *association* of the traditional bourgeois sphere are replaced with an ˌdeologically powerful *homogenization*, an *ersatz* sociality which is little more than the levelling effect of the commodity. The bourgeois public sphere was never, of course, a simple mediation of private experience into public forms, for it was precisely public forms – political, ethical, religious, judicial – which constructed that private experience in the first place. Even so, once subjective experience drawn from the 'intimate' sphere had achieved discursive articulation through the structures of the public sphere, it was able to some extent to operate as a political force, a solid weight of public opinion which might sway the decisions of state. From this viewpoint, the contemporary culture industry appears as a gross caricature of the classical public sphere, drawing upon authentic personal experience, rearticulating it in its own idioms, and returning that message to its consumers in ways which lock them more deeply into a privatized world. 'Capital cannot speak,' writes Brenkman, 'but it can accumulate and concentrate itself in communications media, events and objects which are imbued with this power to turn the discourses of collective experience into a discourse that reconstitutes intersubjectivity as seriality.'[122]

This process, needless perhaps to say, is in no sense inevitable or non-contradictory. The 'mass-mediated public sphere', as Brenkman calls it, does not perpetuate itself, but 'is formed only as it continually appropriates, dismantles, and reassembles the signifying practices of social groups.' Neither a Frankfurtian defeatism nor Enzensbergerian triumphalism is therefore appropriate. What surely *is* true is that no examination of criticism's relation to the classical public sphere can end without considering its relation to the contemporary caricatured form of that sphere, the culture industry. Just as the eighteenth-century bourgeois critic found a role in the cultural politics of the public sphere, so the contemporary socialist or feminist critic must be defined by an engagement in the cultural politics of late capitalism. Both strategies are equally remote from an isolated concern with the 'literary text'. 'The constructing of a proletarian public sphere,' Brenkman argues, ' . . . requires a persistent struggle against the symbolic forms by which the mass-mediated public sphere constitutes subjectivity and puts it under the dominance of the commodity.'[123] The role of the contemporary critic is to resist that dominance by re-connecting the symbolic to the political, engaging through both discourse and practice with the process by which repressed needs, interests and desires may assume the cultural forms which could weld them into a collective political force.

The role of the contemporary critic, then, is a *traditional* one. The point of the present essay is to recall criticism to its traditional role, not to invent some fashionable new function for it. For a new generation of critics in Western society, 'English Literature' is now an inherited label for a field within which many diverse preoccupations congregate: semiotics, psychoanalysis, film studies, cultural theory, the representation of gender, popular writing, and of course the conventionally valued writings of the past. These pursuits have no obvious unity beyond a concern with the symbolic processes of social life, and the social production of forms of subjectivity. Critics who find such pursuits modish and distastefully new-fangled are, as a matter of cultural history, mistaken. They represent a contemporary version of the most venerable topics of criticism, before it was narrowed and impoverished to the so-called 'literary canon'. Moreover, it is possible to argue that such an enquiry might contribute in a modest way to our very survival. For it is surely becoming apparent that without a more profound understanding of such symbolic processes, through which political power is deployed, reinforced, resisted, at times subverted, we shall be incapable of unlocking the most lethal power-struggles now confronting us. Modern criticism was born of a struggle against the absolutist state; unless its future is now defined as a struggle against the bourgeois state, it might have no future at all.

Notes

1. See Jürgen Habermas, *Strukturwandel der Öffentlichkeit*, Neuwied, 1962.

2. *Essays*, ed. William P. Ker, Oxford 1926, p.228.

3. Peter Uwe Hohendahl, *The Institution of Criticism*, Ithaca and London 1982, p.52.

4. L.A. Elioseff, *The Cultural Milieu of Addison's Literary Criticism*, Austin, Texas 1963, p.48. For an account of Addison's political beliefs of a blandness matched only by Addison's own, see E.A. and L.D. Bloom, *Joseph Addison's Sociable Animal*, Providence, Rhode Island 1971.

5. A.J. Beljame, *Men of Letters and the English Public in the Eighteenth Century*, London 1931 p.293.

6. Leslie Stephen, *English Literature and Society in the Eighteenth Century*, London 1963, p.33.

7. Hohendahl, p.53.

8. J.W. Saunders, *The Profession of English Letters*, London 1964, p. 121.

9. Beljame, p.164.

10. W.J. Courthope, *Addison*, London 1884, p.4.

11. Beljame, p. 315.

12. Quoted in Timothy P. Foley, 'Taste and Social Class', unpublished M.S.

13. Quoted in ibid.

14. Quoted in ibid.

15. A.S. Collins, *Authorship in the Days of Johnson*, London 1927, p.240.

16. Jane Jack, 'The Periodical Essayists', in *the Pelican Guide to English Literature, vol. 4: From Dryden to Johnson*, Harmondsworth 1957, p.217.

17. Op.cit, p.44.

18. Richard P. Bond, *The Tatler: The Making of a Literary Journal*,

Cambridge, Mass. 1971, pp. 125-6.

19. Ibid., p.128.

20. William Hazlitt, *Complete Works,* ed. P.P. Howe, London 1931, vol. 6, p.91.

*Op. cit, p.52

21. Quoted by Ian Watt, *The Rise of the Novel,* Harmondsworth 1966, p. 53.

22. Richard Rorty, *The Consequences of Pragmatism,* Minnesota 1982, p.67.

23. Pat Rogers, 'Introduction: The Writer and Society' in *The Eighteenth Century,* ed. Pat Rogers, London 1978, p.46.

24. Stephen, p.23.

25. Thomas Macaulay, 'Life and Writings of Addison', in *Miscelleneous Essays,* vol. 2, London n.d., p. 386.

26. Ibid., p. 440.

27. P. Legouis and L. Cazamian, *A History of English Literature,* London 1957, p.779.

28. Walter Graham, *English Literary Periodicals,* New York 1930, pp. 83-4.

29. See Terry Eagleton, *The Rape of Clarissa,* Oxford 1982, Introduction.

30. Pat Rogers, 'Pope and his Subscribers', *Publishing History* 3 (1978), pp. 7-36.

31. Susan Staves, 'Refinement', unpublished paper.

32. Stephen, p.51.

33. Watt, p.53.

34. Quoted by Watt, p.55.

35. William Hazlitt, op.cit., p.102.

36. Stephen, p.93.

37. G.S. Marr, *The Periodical Essayists of the Eighteenth Century,* London 1923, p.131.

38. Stephen, p.88.

39. Joseph Wood Krutch, *Samuel Johnson,* London 1948, p.88.

40. John Barrell, *English Literature in History 1730-80: An Equal, Wide Survey,* London 1983, p.34.

41. Vicesimus Knox, quoted by Foley, op.cit.

42. Marr, p.226.

43. John Clive, *Scotch Reviewers: The Edinburgh Review 1802-1815,* London 1957, p.122.

44. See Edmund Blunden, *Leigh Hunt's 'Examiner' Examined,* London 1928.

45. See R.G. Cox, 'The Reviews and Magazines' in *Pelican Guide to English Literature vol.6: From Dickens to Hardy,* Harmondsworth 1958, pp. 188-204.

46. *Leigh Hunt's Literary Criticism,* ed. L.H. and C.W. Houtchens,

New York 1976, p. 387.
47. Ibid., p.88.
48. Ibid., p.88.
49. Ibid., p. 381.
50. H.G. Robinson, 'On the use of English Classical Literature in the Work of Education', *Macmillan's Magazine* 11 (1860).
51. Quoted in John Gross, *The Rise and Fall of the Man of Letters*, London 1969, p.16.
52. Quoted in Louis Dudek, *Literature and the Press: A History of Printing, Printed Media and their Relation to Literature*, Toronto 1960, p.212.
53. Quoted in Gross, p.28.
54. See T.W. Heyck, *The Transformation of Intellectual Life in Victorian England*, London 1982, p.13.
55. See Thomas Carlyle, On *Heroes, Hero-Worship and the Heroic in History*, London 1841.
56. Heyck, p.42.
57. ibid., pp. 36-7.
58. Stephen, p.56.
59. Leslie Stephen, *Hours in a Library*, vol. 2, London 1892, p.257.
60. Heyck, pp. 37-8.
61. Quoted in Clive, p. 128.
62. *The National Review*, October 1855; reprinted in *Walter Bagehot: Literary Studies*, ed. R.H. Hutton, vol. 1, London 1902, pp. 146-7.
63. John Morley, *Recollections*, vol. 1, London 1917, p. 100.
64. Samuel Johnson, 'Life of Addison', in *Lives of the English Poets*, ed. G. Birkbeck Hill, vol.2, Oxford 1945, p.132.
65. John Stuart Mill, *On Liberty*, London 1901, pp.138-9.
66. John Stuart Mill, 'Bentham', in *Mill on Bentham and Coleridge*, ed. F.R. Leavis, London 1950, p.89.
67. Quoted by Gross, p.74.
68. Stephen, p.115.
69. Ibid.
70. Ibid., p.43.
71. See Guinevere Griest, *Mudie's Circulating Library and the Victorian Novel*, Bloomington, Ind. 1970.
72. Quoted in Heyck, p.38.
73. John Morley, quoted by Walter Houghton, 'Periodical Literature and the Articulate Classes', in *The Victorian Periodical Press: Samplings and Soundings*, ed. J. Shattock and M. Wolff, Leicester 1982, p.13.
74. M.M. Bevington, *The Saturday Review 1855-1868*, New York 1941, p.47.
75. Christopher Kent,'Higher Journalism and the Mid-Victorian Clerisy', *Victorian Studies* XIII (1969), p.181.

76. Ibid., p. 183.

77. See Arnold's comments on the *Saturday Review* in 'The Literary Influence of Academies'.

78. 'The Function of Criticism at the Present Time', in John Bryson (ed), *Matthew Arnold: Poetry and Prose*, London 1954, pp.359-60.

79. Walter Benjamin, *One-Way Street and Other Essays*, London 1979, p.66.

80. Stephen, p.44.

81. Matthew Arnold, 'The Popular Education of France', in *Democratic Education*, ed. R.H. Super, Ann Arbor 1962, p.26.

82. See J. Hillis Miller, *The Disappearance of God*, New York 1965, p.257.

83. Matthew Arnold, 'The Literary Influence of Academies', p.252.

84. Terry Eagleton, *Literary Theory: An Introduction*, Oxford 1983, Chapter 1.

85. Heyck, p.228.

86. Hohendahl, p.55.

87. Barrell, p.38.

88. Ibid., pp. 40, 41.

89. Elizabeth Bruss, *Beautiful Theories: The Spectacle of Discourse in Contemporary Criticism*, Baltimore and London 1982, pp.30-31.

90. F.R. Leavis, 'Johnson and Augustanism', in *The Common Pursuit*, Harmondsworth 1962, p.103.

91. Ibid., p.114.

92. Ibid., p.110.

93. Ibid., pp.104-5.

94. Ibid., p.103.

95. Ibid., pp. 103-4.

96. F.R. Leavis, 'English Poetry in the Eighteenth Century', *Scrutiny* vol. V, 1, June 1936, p.22.

97. 'Johnson and Augustanism', p.111.

98. Denys Thompson, 'Prospects for a Weekly', *Scrutiny II*, 3, December 1933, p.250.

99. R.G. Cox, 'The Great Reviews', *Scrutiny VI*, 2, September 1937, p. 175.

100. F.R. Leavis, *For Continuity*, London 1933, p.72.

101. Francis Mulhern, *The Moment of 'Scrutiny'*, London 1979, p.326.

102. Hohendahl, p.55.

103. Quoted in Hohendahl, p.165.

104. Bruss, pp. 16-17.

105. Ibid., p.17.

106. Quoted in Bruss, p.19.

107. See Fredric Jameson, 'Pleasure: A Political Issue', in *Formations of Pleasure*, London 1983, p.5.

108. Terry Eagleton, *Walter Benjamin, or Towards a Revolutionary Criticism*, London 1981, pp. 137-8.

109. Paul de Man, *Blindness and Insight*, Minnesota 1983, p.214.

110. Paul A. Bové, 'Variations on Authority', in *The Yale Critics: Deconstruction in America*, ed. J. Arac, W. Godzich and W. Martin, Minnesota 1983, p.6.

111. Quoted by Bové, p.11.

112. Peter Hohendahl, 'The Use Value of Contemporary and Future Literary Criticism', *New German Critique* 7, winter 1976, p.7.

113. See Robert Weimann, *Structure and Society*, London 1977, especially Chapter 2.

114. Raymond Williams, *Politics and Letters*, London 1979, pp. 73-4.

115. Ibid., p. 106.

116. Nicos Poulantzas, *State, Power, Socialism*, London 1978, p.72.

117. See Oskar Negt and Alexander Kluge, *Öffentilichkeit und Erfahrung: Zur Organisationsanalyse von bürgerlicher and proletarischer Offentlichkeit*, Frankfurt/Main, 1972.

118. John Brenkman, 'Mass Media: From Collective Experience to the Culture of Privatization', *Social Text* 1, Winter 1979, p. 94.

119. Ibid., p.95.

120. Ibid., p.98.

121. Ibid., p. 105.

122. Ibid.

123. Ibid., p. l08.

Index

133